....(Full Reviews on www.timothysykes.com)

Comparisons:

"A clearly-written account of a natural trader coming of age, a *Catcher in the Rye* for traders. Highly recommend"
-Aaron C. Brown. *Face of Wall Street*

"Want the ride of your life? It reads like *Reminiscences of a Stock Operator*...Tim holds nothing back..."
-Alexander Paul Morris, President of Yourika Corp., *MoMoneyTV.com*

"Updates *Reminiscences of a Stock Operator* into the 21st Century..."
-Allan Harris, *AllAllan.Blogspot.com*

"*The Da Vinci Code* for investors. Every turn of the page is more engrossing..."
-Andy Swan, Founder and CEO, MyTrade.com

"Should be read by anyone who is serious about making money trading...reminds me of *How I Made $2 Million in the Stock Market* and *Reminiscences of a Stock Operator*..."
-Brian Shannon, *AlphaTrends.Blogspot.com*

"The most realistic portrayal of the risks, rewards, joys, frustrations, exhilarations and the depths of a trader's life since *Reminiscences of a Stock Operator*."
-Craig L Howe, Faulkner and me, Amazon Top 500 Reviewer

"Potentially the new *Reminiscences of a Stock Operator* as it's definitely a future classic in this genre..."
-Dave Goodboy, *TradingMarkets.com*

"I could hardly put it down! Right up there with *Confessions of a Street Addict* as one of my all-time favorite books about stock traders..."
-Fred Fuld III, *StockerBlog.com*

"Not since *How I Made $2 Million in the Stock Market* has anyone written such a personal and extremely informative account of their trading experience...a must read..."
-J. Lauriston, *The Lauriston Letter*

"Not since *Dumb Money* have I found...sarcastic humor and no-holds-barred honesty so authentic and compelling..."
-Jeff White, Founder, *TheStockBandit.net*

"Finally! A follow-up to the classics, *Reminiscences of a Stock Operator* and *How I Made $2 Million in the Stock Market*...a must read for any aspiring trader..."
-Kevin Kelly, *BloggingStocks.com*

"I can't believe I've finished the whole book in less than 24 hours...last time I had this same enthusiasm about a book was when I read *The Secret*..."
-Noel Bautista, *2MinuteCommute.com*

"The modern-day *Reminiscences of a Stock Operator*..."
-Ron Sen, *Ronsen.Blogspot.com*

"This is the 21st century's *Reminiscences of a Stock Operator*...READ IT!"
-Shuo Liu, *UCLATrader.Blogspot.com*

"This is the modern-day *Reminiscences of a Stock Operator*. A wonderful insight into the often mystical world of day-trading and hedge funds."
-Theo Wong, *StokBlogs.com*

"One of the few books besides *Reminiscences of a Stock Operator* that I read cover-to-cover non-stop..."
-Victor William, *BuzzingBell.com*

Business Leaders:

"Should be a prerequisite for every kid coming out of business school…"
-Adrian James, President, The Stockwire Group

"Tim's story and his honesty will inspire generations to come."
-Brett Fogle, CEO, Options University

"This book isn't just about making money; it's an inspirational yet realistic look at the world of trading and startup hedge funds."
-Chad Brand, President, Peridot Capital Management, LLC and author of *The Peridot Capitalist*

"A must read for every man, woman, and child who wishes to get into the world of hedge funds."
-Chris Lahiji, Founder of LD Micro

"Tim captures the mindset and drive of the at-home, chart-based stock trader…you'll find this book eye-opening…"
-David Jackson, Founder and CEO, Seeking Alpha

"Masterfully crafts inspirational lessons about trading and life as a must-read guide for everybody pursuing the American Dream."
-Dr. Prieur du Plessis, CEO of Plexus Asset Management, *InvestmentPostCards.com*

"A must read for entrepreneurs everywhere…"
-Evan Carmichael, Founder, Evan Carmichael Communications Group

"This is the first book I'd give to somebody if I were trying to interest them in the stock market…"
-Greg Feirman, Founder and CEO, Top Gun Financial Planning

"Brutal honesty and self-criticism…is what distinguishes this book from others…"
-Jeffrey Mishlove, PhD, President, Intuition Network, *ForecastingSystems.com*

"Should be required reading for anyone contemplating an investment in a startup…"
-Kenneth Wasserman, President, ASKM, LLC

"A no holds barred and hilarious look…honest reflection…a great read for all…"
-Matt Brown, Founder, Investors Hub

"I love the book… it's a very honest portrayal of one man's journey…"
-Neal Berger, President, Eagle's View Asset Management, LLC

"A surprise for veteran or beginner…Mr. Sykes exposes a lot of himself which allows you to see the development of the trading mind…"
-Online Trading Academy

"What a great book. Engaging, honest and entertaining…"
-Perry Blacher, Cofounder, Covestor

"This will be a big hit with college students and inspire many."
-Peter Ricchiuti, Assistant Dean, Professor of Finance, Freeman School of Business, Tulane University

"A must read for anyone dreaming of becoming a hedge fund manager…"
-Sam Butler, President, Steadfast Resource Associates

"A highly-entertaining and riveting account…a must-read for all aspiring traders and hedge fund managers…"
-Stephen Karl, Founder of *Stockalicious.com*

"A story that will inspire the next generation of investors…"
-Thomas Catino, Managing Member, Ant & Sons LLC

"A clear, unbiased view of trading…many lessons…I highly recommend it…"
-Tom Alexander, Partner, Alexander Trading, Savannah River Capital Management

"A refreshing perspective from one of the industry's rising young stars—it even draws a little blood…"
-Tom Sosnoff, Cofounder and CEO, Thinkorswim, Inc.

Authors:

"A fun and entertaining read about one of Wall Street's most important subjects."
-Daniel Strachman, Managing Partner, A & C Advisors LLC, Author
of *The Fundamentals of Hedge Fund Management*

"A professional trader myself, I can totally identify...I find it absolutely inspirational..."
-Grace Cheng, *GraceCheng.com*, Author of *7 Winning Strategies For Trading Forex*

"Tim lays it on the line. The pain, the hunger, the glory, the brutality of trading
in the trenches. Read this before you try to turn $12,000 into $2,000,000."
-James Altucher, President, Stockpickr LLC, Formula Capital, and
Author of *Trade Like a Hedge Fund* and *SuperCa$h*

"Entertaining, insightful, and educational...it's a great read..."
-Jame 'RevShark' Deporre, President, SharkInvesting.com, Author of *Invest Like a Shark*

"An interesting story that any trader will appreciate..."
-John Boik, Author of *Lessons from the Greatest Stock Traders of All
Time* and *How Legendary Traders Made Millions*

"A book all aspiring traders should read. The mental elements of trading described
in Tim's story, both positive and negative, are ones that all traders experience..."
-John Forman, Author of *The Essentials of Trading*

"The government doesn't want you listening to Timothy Sykes. That's why you should."
-Michael Covel, Bestselling Author of *The Complete TurtleTrader* and *Trend Following*

"Of all the trading books I have read, this is one of the most entertaining, honest
and applicable..."
-Peter Leeds, Author of *Understanding Penny Stocks, PennyStocks.com*

"A breath of fresh air. I read it cover to cover in one sitting and didn't get bored for a moment..."
-Russell Bailyn, Author of *Navigating the Financial Blogosphere*

"A pulse-quickening, insider's view of an incredible time in market history..."
-Tim Knight, Founder, *Prophet.net*, *Slope-Of-Hope.com* and Author of *Chart Your Way To Profits*

"An engaging story about a talented day trader...his success and ultimate clarity of
purpose is inspiring..."
-Tracy L. Coenen, Author of *Essentials of Corporate Fraud, Sequence-Inc.com*

"A wonderful, entertaining, frank tale of how randomness met Wall Street."
-Vitaliy Katsenelson, Author of *Active Value Investing: Making Money in Range Bound Markets*

Financial Journalists:

"An honest look at the world of trading, control and "easy" money..."
-Alex Akesson, Editor, *Hedgeco.net*

"If you think you're about to read a boring business book, think again...you won't be able
to put it down..."
-Alice Berger, *Muse Reviews*

"I loved this book...I highly recommend this book to anyone who is interested in...the stock market..."
-Amy Allen Clark, *MomAdvice.com*

"Fresh perspective on trading small caps...don't let (Tim's) age fool you..."
-Andrew Coffey, Reporter, *MN1.com*

"Very enjoyable and readable...American-style..."
-Ashkan Karbasfrooshan, *WatchMojo.com*

"An honest look at one person's attempt to succeed on his own terms..."
-*BelowTheCrowd.com*

"A brutally honest assessment...a revealing look..."
-Bill Rempel, *BillakaNoDoodahs.com*

"A fascinating personal account offering compelling insights into an often poorly understood industry."
-*FreeMoneyFinance.com*

"Why 26-year-olds who write autobiographies probably shouldn't bother actually publishing them..."
-Greg Newton, *NakedShorts*

"Timothy...even includes his negative qualities—this candidness is refreshing..."
-*HighChartPatterns.com*

"Investor or trader, this is a must read...it will re-energize your trading and entrepreneurial spirits..."
-Himanshu Pandya, *FinancialNirvana.com*

"Honest and straightforward...a lasting impression of what is possible and how nothing is guaranteed..."
-Jack Fyfe, *StockLogic.Blogspot.com*

"A highly engaging read that cuts right to the core of the human condition..."
-Jarrett Hailes, Founder, *Investoid.com*

"Every stock blogger should read this book..."
-Jason Brietstein, *StockRake.com*

"Nothing short of inspirational. We may be witnesses to a Trading Legend in the making..."
-Jay Harbans, Owner & Chief Trader, *BannRonn.com*

"In a voice filled with both honesty and passion, Timothy entertains us..."
-Jay Walker, *The Confused Capitalist*

"Can help you avoid the true pitfalls of trading and startups in general..."
-Jimmy Huen, *FoundersCafe.com*

"Presents keen insights into navigating volatile markets...gives great guidance on avoiding pitfalls..."
-Jim Kingsland, Market Columnist, *CNBC.com*

"A story about how hard work and determination can bring back the American dream..."
-Jim Wang, *Bargaineering.com*

"An important lesson hidden in this book is how a trader can...remain in the game..."
-Joey Fundora, *DowntownTrader.Blogspot.com*

"One of the best books I've read all year. Timothy serves as an inspiration to all young traders...a must read."
-John Chow, *JohnChow.com*

"Similar to a great adventure story or mystery where you can't wait to see how it all ends..."
-Joseph Meth, S*tockChartist.Blogspot.com*

"A pioneering look into the hedge fund industry...I am inspired to redouble my own efforts..."
-Joshua Cyr, *SpamStockTracker.com*

"A fascinating account of a trader, but more importantly an entrepreneur...a must read..."
-Justin Lenarcic, Alpha Advisor

"Nothing short of riveting for anyone with a passion for the American dream."
-Karen E. Spaeder, Entrepreneur, Former Managing Editor of Entrepreneur

"A true coming-of-age story...filled with real-life anecdotes...a must read..."
-Keith Lau, Founder, *TippingMonkey.com*

"Takes you on a refreshing, easy-to-read tour...Enjoy it!"
-Larry Hoffenberg, *BearMarketCentral.com*

"If ever there was a straight forward, get to know what the market is all about book, this is that book..."
-Lea Schizas, Founder, Muse Book Reviews

"Tim's honesty in portraying his story makes for a memorable, inspiring read for anyone..."
-Lloyd Sakazaki, *LloydsInvestment.Blogspot.com*

"I finished the book with a big smile on my face! Timothy gives some very good tips..."
-*MaddMoney.Blogspot.com*

"A must read for anyone who aspires to be a real trader or hedge fund manager..."
-Manoj Agrawal, *OptionPundit.com*

"A captivating story that reminds us we can make something of ourselves..."
-Matthew Paulson, *FinanceIsPersonal.com*

"Takes you into the game showing you what it takes to become a master..."
-*Market-Speculator.com*

"A must read for young entrepreneurs...it almost feels like you're in the game..."
-Marshall Middle, *HowToMakeAMillionDollars.com*

"Big Losses...Big Gains...Big Lessons..."
-Michael Steinhardt, *HEDGEFolios.com*

"A true coming of age story...Tim's honesty is something all traders can learn from..."
-Michael Taylor, *TaylorTree.com*

"If you love the markets, you will love this story..."
-*Microcapspeculator.net*

"Truly inspirational...revealing insights...a must read...highly recommended..."
-*Milliondollarjourney.com*

"If you're a stock trader, this book is a must read and a great addition to your library..."
-*MyShareTrading.com*

"It's refreshing...I couldn't help but get excited..."
-Neville Medhora, *NevBlog.com*

"Absolutely riveting!"
-Nirav Desai, *MoneyShaker.Blogspot.com*

"I feel inspired...this book helped open my eyes to the possibilities that are out there..."
-*OneBadTradeBlogspot.com*

"No crap, no bullship, a first hand look into the hedge fund industry..."
-Oskar Syahbana, *Permagnus.com*

"I was captivated...and spent far too many nights tossing and turning with my eyes glued to this book..."
-P. Michell Mayo, *Audeamus.com*

"The breathtaking trading life of a successful speculator..."
-Paolo Pezzutti, *Short-TermTrading.Blogspot.com*

"One of the most exciting reads about a trader's journey...a must read..."
-*PinoyTrader.Blogspot.com*

"An immensely enjoyable, gripping yarn that provides a rare glimpse inside the US hedge fund industry..."
-Ralph Morgan, *EnoughWealth.com*

"This begins as a fun, first-hand account...goes on to combine trading stories with a rare inside look..."
-Richard Todd, *MoveTheMarkets.com*

"Part autobiography, part trading diary, part industry expose, it's unique...both entertaining and educational..."
-Rob May, *BusinessPundit.com*

"Will be thoroughly enjoyed by experienced traders and new investors alike..."
-Rob Rizzoni, *StockDollars.Blogspot.com*

"This is a great read for young people looking to get into the finance industry."
-Roger Nusbaum, *RandomRoger.Blogspot.com*

"Elegant style...personifies the entrepreneurial challenges and rewards..."
-Sam Huleatt, *LeveragingIdeas.com*

"Tim illustrates his excitingly true story...while shedding light on the controversial hedge fund industry..."
-*SmallCapsLargeGains.com*

"Tim provides a detailed account of how he followed through on his dreams...an inspiration for all college investors."
-Stefan McVeigh, *College-Investor.com*

"A testament to all who strive to enter this unforgiving business...I highly recommend it!"
-Steve Todoroff, *SogoTrading.Blogspot.com*

"I was fascinated...Tim's talent as a trader shines through in this book...will be considered a classic..."
-*SqueezeShorts.Blogspot.com*

"Takes us on the rollercoaster of emotions...a firm reminder of what happens when hard work and passion collide..."
-Tate Dwinnell, *SelfInvestors.com*

"An engaging real life tale...exposes the realities startup hedge funds face..."
-*TheTradingDigest.com*

"Definitely worth reading if you've ever dabbled in day trading..."
-Thomas Duff, *TWDuff.com*, Amazon Top 100 Reviewer

"This is Jim Cramer on steroids that will make many older legends of years past run to the bathroom for their Depends..."
-Tom Smicklas, *InvestingFromTheRight.Blogspot.com*

"A modern day, page turner...will, no doubt, motivate many aspiring traders. Highly recommended!"
-*TraderJamie.Blogspot.com*

"The life of a trader is fun...nothing exemplifies this better than this book..."
-*WallStreetFighter.com*

"Proves that anybody with a good strategy can beat the Wall Street pros..."
-Winston Kotzan, *WinstonKotzan.com*

"A fun read..."
-William Trent, CFA, *StockMarketBeat.com*

"Highly entertaining as Timothy does a great job of telling his story..."
-*WylieMoney.com*

"With the allure of hedge funds, the sizzle of a Silicon Valley start-up, this is a lucid review..."
-Yaser Anwar, *YaserAnwar.com*

"Enjoyable and eye opening. Tim's transparency...make this a recommended read..."
-*YourTradingStock.com*

"A must-read for every stock-market junkie who has ever dreamed of having their own hedge fund..."
-Zac Bissonnnette, *BloggingStocks.com*

Anonymous:

Visit www.timothysykes.com

- To learn about Timothy's instructional trading DVD: **PennyStocking** (BullShip-free, Money-Back Guaranteed)

- To see detailed charts of the trades mentioned (As denoted by the *(t)* icon throughout the book)

- To sign-up to Timothy's Newsletter

- To read Timothy's blog

- To discover Freedom of Finance

- To view Timothy's favorite websites, blogs and books

- To watch exclusive video clips

- To enjoy exclusive offers on future products from BullShip Press

- To read free articles by Timothy and other experts

An American Hedge Fund

How I Made $2 Million as a Stock Operator
&
Created a Hedge Fund

Timothy Sykes

BullShip Press, LLC

Hamden, CT

For copies and further information, address to:
BullShip Press, LLC, 900 Mix Ave., Unit 22, Hamden, CT 06514

First Edition

Book design by: Vu Cao
Edited by: Alexander Paul Morris, Allison Kaye and Paula Plantier

Sykes, Timothy; An American Hedge Fund: How I Made $2 Million as a Stock Operator and
Created a Hedge Fund

ISBN 10: 0-9795497-0-1
ISBN 13: 978-0-9795497-0-0

Library of Congress Control Number: 2007903520
Library of Congress subject heading: Hedge Funds, Investments, Speculation, Stocks

Disclaimer

This book was not designed to provide more than anecdotal information on stock trading and hedge funds. It is sold with the understanding that the publisher and author are not engaged in rendering legal, accounting, professional or investment advice of any kind. If legal or other expert assistance is required, the reader should see the services of a competent professional.

It is not the purpose of this material to reprint the investment information that is otherwise available to traders, fund managers and the public but instead to relay one individual's experiences in the finance industry. You are urged to read all available material, learn as much as possible about stock trading and fund managing, and tailor the information to your individual needs with the assistance of trained professionals as may be necessary.

Trading and, more specifically, hedge funds are not "get-rich-quick" schemes. Serious pursuit of the activities described in this book requires a great deal of time and energy in order to learn the intricacies of the marketplace. Even then, there are no guarantees of success, as many hardworking people involved in these activities still lose money.

Every effort has been made to make this book as complete and accurate as possible. However, there may be typographical and/or factual errors and omissions. Therefore, this text should be used only for entertainment purposes and not as a reference for trading and hedge fund information. Furthermore, this book contains trading and hedge fund information that is current only up to the first printing date.

The purpose of this book is to entertain. The author and BullShip Press, LLC shall not be held liable for any loss or damage caused or alleged to have been caused, directly or indirectly to any person and/or entity, by the information contained in this book. Any mischaracterizations or misrepresentations of people, places or organizations are done unintentionally and without malice.

If you do not wish to be bound by the above, the author and BullShip Press, LLC kindly request that you please stop reading this book now.

Contents

Acknowledgements

Acknowledgements

I would like to thank the thousands of inept corporate management teams, shady brokers, boiler rooms, pump and dumpers, stock promoters, market manipulators, wannabe traders, newsletter writers and Internet message board posters—for your endless scheming and undying greed, without which my fortune would never have been possible. Thank you to the third-party marketers, accredited investors, hedge fund databases, TV producers, journalists, bloggers, CNBC and, of course, the SEC, for without you my story would probably never have been told. Most importantly, I have to thank the people who gave me money for my bar mitzvah, for unwittingly being my first investors, and my parents, for willfully investing in me and supporting me in all my endeavors.

Hedge Fund

A mutual fund organized as a limited partnership and using high-risk, speculative methods to obtain large profits.
—*Dictionary.com*

An investment company that uses high-risk techniques—such as borrowing money and selling short—in an effort to make extraordinary capital gains.
—*American Heritage Dictionary*

A flexible investment company for a small number of large investors (usually requiring a minimum investment of $1 million); can use high-risk techniques (not allowed for mutual funds) such as short selling and heavy leveraging.
—*WordNet, Princeton University*

An investing group usually in the form of a limited partnership that employs speculative techniques in the hope of obtaining large capital gains.
—*Merriam-Webster's Collegiate Dictionary*

Introduction

I have no extraordinary talents and yet I was a millionaire by the age of 22. I was raised to believe in America and in all of our nation's most sacred principles, including freedom, justice and success through hard work. I created my wealth by repeatedly betting much of what I had in the belief that I could predict the future of certain stocks' prices. I was right often enough to become wealthy within a few years. Most people are reluctant to talk about how much they earn, while my profession is defined by it. Most people mismanage money; my wealth is built on the backs of other people's financial mismanagement. I take from the middle and upper classes and give to myself. I get paid only if I can correctly predict how a stock will act over the next few minutes, hours and days.

I am a stock trader and I earn a living from trading the smallest, most volatile publicly-traded companies in America. There is no salary, no pension, no health insurance, not even any coworkers, but the independence of it all is exhilarating. On several occasions, I have lost and gained hundreds of thousands of dollars, all within a few minutes or hours. It is gambling, but it is researched gambling. The digital world has created a new frontier where it's every man for himself—and there are few rules. You either make money or you don't. It's the American dream on steroids.

I made huge amounts of money for years and then tried to expand my operation by becoming a hedge fund manager. Yes, I became part of the vaulted high-stakes end of the investment business that has recently become the center of much debate. I had no idea what I was getting myself into. This was a whole new ballgame and I was about to receive quite an education. The industry was subject to U.S. Securities and Exchange Commission (SEC) regulations that prohibited advertising, talking to the press and any detailing of business activity to non-wealthy people. These regulations were designed to protect investors who had no business investing in hedge funds, but instead, they have hurt only the smallest of funds like mine. Industry growth has continued unabated, but due to the lack of publicly available information, the media has gotten it wrong and the general public has become scared and confused. This has made it nearly impossible for startup funds with few connections to raise capital. There are reasons why 80% of the money invested in hedge funds is controlled by 20% of the funds, and much of it is due to industry regulations.

This great country was built by people who risked everything for a chance at a new future, success and freedom. Hedge fund managers share similar dreams. Some are successful, but many more are not. Win or lose, industry regulations prohibit us from telling our stories, so the press reports on industry corruption and failure, creating skepticism among investors. The media has detailed only this industry's greatest failures, while everything else is pure guesswork, unable to be confirmed or denied by its subjects. Every industry has derelicts, and yet ours are paraded in front of the masses, skewing public perception.

My hedge fund is little more than a speck in this colossal industry, and yet it serves as a shining example of why hedge funds should be free of oppressive restrictions. The word *speculator* should not have a negative connotation. We represent the very definition of entrepreneurship and the American dream. If we win, we're richer, and if we lose, we're wiser. If you can afford to play, it really is a great profession. Financial speculation is in every American's blood; it's our true national sport and we should be free to discuss it in detail. Nothing less than the very right of free speech is at stake here. Some might argue the American system of free trade is at risk, too. The general public, including many people in the investment community itself, has never heard the truth about this industry. This needs to change.

Throughout my financial journey, I made plenty of mistakes, but I will not commit the ultimate blunder by not giving others the opportunity to learn from my experiences. Rich or poor, all people have a right to hear about financial speculation and hedge funds. I can no longer sit back and allow the public's misconception of financial speculators to continue. It is time for somebody on the inside to talk about their experiences in detail. My disillusionment with the hedge fund industry is actually a blessing in disguise, because I am now free to tell my story.

I write to inspire, entertain, caution, and, most importantly, educate society about this incredible profession. Think about it: if such inaccuracies can be spread about the entrepreneurial spirit of the up-and-coming hedge fund industry, what's next? I hope this book will serve as a rallying cry for all of us so we can protect our basic right to discuss our businesses with whoever shows interest.

Stock trading is my life, and yet, due to industry regulations, I have been forced to turn away thousands of people who have been inspired by my story. Sure, most could not afford to invest in my fund, but they probably knew somebody who would be interested. Now I will never know. A startup company needs to talk to as many people as possible, because it needs to quickly raise capital or else it will probably fail. The key to raising capital is networking, and when industry regulations prevent startups from doing so, fundraising becomes much more difficult.

More importantly, the incredible lack of freely available information regarding financial speculation and hedge funds hurts society as a whole. Industry regulations have created an environment that is ripe for fraud and manipulation, which leads to unnecessary losses, not to mention it hinders people's abilities to learn from past successes and failures. These are the dark ages for hedge funds.

No longer will I play by these misguided rules. I should be free to discuss my business, for I am an American entrepreneur. I call this *freedom of finance*. Freedom of finance is the concept of a hedge fund manager's right to discuss business freely without fear of penalty or censorship. I practice what I preach; this is my story.

Timothy Sykes
July 4, 2007

Prologue: A View from the Top

I was about to enter one of the most revered offices in the entire financial industry. This company's $4-billion hedge fund was headed by a trader who'd recently been profiled in a major business publication as the best trader on Wall Street. His personal net worth was now over $1 billion, and on any given day he accounted for nearly 3% of the entire market's trading volume. As a fledging hedge fund manager, this trader and his firm represented everything I aspired to one day become.

But I wasn't going there for a job. I intended to pitch them for an investment to help grow my fund. And $10 million was all I needed—an insignificant investment for them, a huge jump-start for me. Of course, the legitimacy of being connected to their hugely successful organization was part of the package as well. Success by association is the name of the game in the secretive hedge fund world.

One of my industry contacts, a fellow Tulane alumnus, worked for this fund. I'd been courting him for months, but only after I donated $1,000 to Tulane's Hillel organization, did he agree to meet with me to discuss my fund in detail at his firm's offices in Stamford, Connecticut. As I made the reverse commute from New York City to Connecticut, crossing the terrain that encompassed the majority of the hedge fund universe, I was actually amazed that my heart was able to beat as fast as it did throughout the hour-long journey. The anticipation was exhilarating.

As I walked into the firm's high-tech, fortress-like brick building, my heart beat faster. I'd worked hard to get to this point, but for all my effort, my tiny fund could barely be considered a hedge fund. I was now one door and one successful pitch away from raising enough capital to fulfill a lifelong dream of becoming a true fund manager.

"Can I help you?" said a security guard, looking up sternly from his desk.

I couldn't talk. No words would come out. I felt beads of sweat form on my forehead as my heart raced.

"Can I help you, sir?" the security guard repeated. "Um, yes. I'm—I'm here to see—um—" and I managed to sputter out my contact's name.

"What's the purpose of your visit?" the guard said, sensing my trepidation.

"Um—I'm—I'm—um—" Again, no words would come out.

Come on, what's wrong with you? How are you ever going to raise millions of dollars from anyone if you're this nervous when you're talking to a security guard?

"Yeah, you just want to get in, right?" said the security guard, smiling. He obviously had experience with this kind of awkwardness. His smile helped calm me down some what.

"Yeah, that's pretty much it," I said as I now joined him in smiling, too.

The guard handed me a visitor's sticky tag. I wrote my name on it with the marker he gave me and then placed it on my suit jacket.

"Wait here," he said, motioning me to a nearby couch. I was surprised to see that this gargantuan firm's security rested on a rent-a-cop and a sticky name tag that could be purchased in any local convenience store. No high-tech photo ID. No closed-circuit TV system. It was just the latest in a long string of surprises I'd already encountered in this strange industry.

My contact's assistant appeared, greeted me, and ushered me to the firm's trading floor. The sight was incredible; the trading floor was as large as an airplane hangar and there were more computer monitors than I'd ever seen in one place before. Hundreds of traders scurried back and forth among them. I could feel the tension and the pressure to perform. What a difference this was from my "operation," which consisted of me dressed in a bathrobe with one computer and three monitors in my SoHo loft.

I was ushered into one of the dozen side offices that surrounded the massive open space in the middle and was told to wait there. Apparently, this was my contact's office. When he strolled in, he was a casually dressed, middle-aged man who seemed surprisingly laid-back considering how much money he probably earned. He introduced himself, made small talk, and eventually brought one of his friends into the compact office to join him in listening to my pitch. I'd already had a dozen or so pitches under my belt, but I was still an amateur, particularly because I enjoyed winging it and seeing the looks of disbelief on the faces of my potential investors when I told them my story. Just a few months out of college, I was earning nearly $40,000 a month from trading and was cockier than ever. Those were some big bucks for me, but peanuts for these guys. Still, they listened intently while making a few notes.

After I finished, they said they liked my trading style and my niche strategy but wouldn't consider investing until I had had a full year of fund performance to show them. That was another eight months away! In that time, I would have dozens maybe hundreds of worthy plays under my belt and everyone would've made tons of money. I tried not to show my frustration. Unfortunately, meetings with large investors like this were rare, so my shot at the big time was over for the time being. I graciously thanked them for their time but thought their judgment overly cautious.

I was surprised when they invited me to stay for lunch. Somehow I thought they'd be too busy researching and trading to spend time eating, let alone spend more time with a small-time trader like me. The three of us headed down to the building's lower level that doubled as the firm's cafeteria. As we walked, my contact explained that each side office represented the research team for every industry that their fund covered. The center of the building was reserved for traders who executed orders based on the various teams' research. My contact's job was to cover the dozen or so major companies in the sector he followed and to know as much as humanly possible about each company.

Talk about specialization. I followed thousands of stocks across dozens of industry sectors; I'd have a lot of free time if I narrowed my trading universe down to a dozen companies. I mentioned how I'd read the recent article about their firm. He laughed and told me that it was extremely inaccurate because the information had come from several disgruntled former employees. As I looked at him to see if he was lying, he quickly asked, "Hey, would you like to meet him?"

I looked at him in astonishment and replied, "Um, of course, of course I'd like to meet him—if it's not too much trouble."

"No, it's no trouble at all. He's probably busy trading, but you can at least say hello," my contact said. This was too much. One hour ago, I could barely speak to the firm's security guard and now I was about to meet the single best trader in the world. Luckily, I didn't have time to get scared because after a few steps, we were already at the billionaire trader's station. The best trader in the world was a distinguished-looking man with thick glasses, whose eyes were completely focused on the dozen computer monitors that surrounded him. Several telephones covered his otherwise neat desk.

"Hey, meet Tim Sykes. He's a young trader with his own little fund," my contact explained. The commentary forced the best trader in the world to slowly turn his head away from the monitors and in my direction as he extended his hand to me. "It's a great honor to meet you," I blurted out as I tried to make sure I shook his hand firmly.

We didn't have time to really make eye contact because just as I shook his hand, one of his telephones rang. He picked it up and turned his attention back to his computer monitors. It was but a brief encounter, but it was an unbelievable moment for me.

I'd met the man who I hoped, with enough hard work, to one day become.

When we got to the downstairs cafeteria, we chose our lunches from the upscale buffet line and sat down at a nearby table. While we ate, I was introduced to several other traders and staff members, with whom I made polite conversation. I was most impressed with one particular person, the firm's on-site trading coach. He was a very polite and inquisitive older gentleman whose knowledge about trading seemed to know no bounds. He was apparently well paid to be on-site in case any trader wanted to talk to him. I knew that many of my largest trading losses had been due to a lack of discipline, and having an experienced coach to talk to probably would've helped a great deal.

While our conversation lasted only a few minutes, he impressed me enough that I made a mental note to purchase all the books my contact told me he'd written. I figured that if a multi-billion-dollar hedge fund believed in his teachings, I could also benefit from them. It would be another step in my quest to grow my operation into a similar kind of empire.

After lunch, I thanked my contact for meeting me and taking the time to listen to my pitch, but I left somewhat disappointed. On the way home, I had a lot to think about. I'd finally seen what a real hedge fund looked like. I knew I'd get there if I worked hard enough and made the right contacts. It was just a matter of time.

The next morning, I noticed the word "VOID" was showing through on the sticky visitor's tag I'd judged as so low-tech the day before. I laughed. It was some kind of advanced name tag that really was ingenious as a security precaution after all. Never underestimate a billionaire.

Chapter 1: Start Me Up

I was raised as a middle-class kid in a small rural town in Connecticut. For as long as I can remember, my parents instilled in me the belief that I was capable of becoming anyone I wanted to be, as long as I worked hard enough to get there. From an early age, I wanted to be rich. My family owned a jewelry store, but I knew that business was not for me. No, I wanted to build my empire from scratch.

When I was nine, I scoured the woods behind the tennis courts of our local country club for lost tennis balls in the hope of selling them later for a profit. The balls were so easy to find that after a few hours, they filled up several large garbage bags. With

my garbage bags in tow, I then went door-to-door in my neighborhood and offered to sell the used tennis balls for a quarter
apiece. I've always been a scrapper and I've never cared who
knew it. I can only imagine what my neighbors thought of this
little scheme. Many of them felt sorry enough to buy some of
those dirty used tennis balls, and I made a few hundred dollars
within a couple of days. I looked at the money and thought, "I
might have a knack for this."

My next money-making venture was much more conven-
tional. In junior high school, I devoted my entire mind, body and
soul to baseball card trading. My friends and I followed every
statistic imaginable, studying the market prices while attempting to gain the upper hand in our dealings. *Beckett Baseball Card
Monthly* was our main source for card prices, so it became our
bible as we studied and memorized it with an almost religious
fervor. The magazine was issued monthly, so we counted the days
until the next issue would arrive. I could hardly wait to see the
updated card prices so I could study and use them as a framework
for future trades.

But my emotions often got in the way of my card-trading dealings. I was a sucker for whatever the hottest card of the moment was,
paying no attention to its long-term value. The newer cards' prices
were very volatile, and I thoroughly enjoyed guessing which way
the volatility would swing next. The value of the cards of the hottest
players seemed to be able to rise for months on end, but I somehow
always became scared and sold much too early. When I invested
in any particular card, it was as if I'd become teammates with the
player but never really trusted him to deliver. I'd sever ties with him
when I sold his card. Every time I sold for a profit, my ego was satis-

fied because it felt great to be right about the investment even if the dollar gain was not as great as it could have been had I just waited.

Even at that young age, it was clear to me that I enjoyed the "action" of the marketplace, and my moneymaking suffered as a result. After a few years of chasing the popular cards and usually selling too early, I decided to go against the grain. I created birthday and holiday wish lists asking relatives to buy the complete sets from the 1980s for me because they contained key rookie cards of the game's best players like Cal Ripken Jr., Roger Clemens and Barry Bonds. These rookies had by now become famous players, and their rookie cards had increased substantially in value. I didn't realize it at the time, but I'd stumbled upon the classic investment strategy of buying and holding blue-chip investments for the long term. I planned to hold these sets for years—decades, if need be—and watch as their value climbed like the highly prized rookie cards of the stars from the 1950s and 1960s.

Unfortunately, the economics of the market had changed since those many decades past. The main reason for the older cards' astronomical prices was their scarcity, a fact that many collectors of my generation failed to take into consideration. In the past, parents routinely discarded their children's old baseball cards along with their old toys because they had no concept of how valuable the cards would one day become. Those lucky enough to have kept their collections intact were rewarded with individual card values that soared into the thousands of dollars.

The newer cards, even those from the 1980s, were massproduced so they were much easier to come by. In the 1980s and 1990s, the children from the 1950s and 1960s were now parents, and they vowed not to make the same mistake twice. So, the newer cards were bought en masse and packed away by many adults who thought they could beat the market this time around. As of yet, the demand for these cards still has not exceeded the massive supply and, as such, their relative value has not increased. This marketplace offered me great lessons in economics, market pricing and supply and demand, but I was too young to benefit from them.

Tennis gave me another basic lesson in business. I began playing tennis when I was six years old. By the time I was in high school, I'd developed a powerful serve, which caused the strings in my rackets to frequently break. The local pro shops charged over $50 to string each racket, and I believed their prices to be excessive. I spent hours researching, trying to find any stringers who'd charge less. But the market was locked; professional stringers all charged similar amounts. The only way to save money in the long run was to buy a stringing machine for myself and buy the string in bulk. After a few months of prodding, my parents gave into my idea of "investing" in a stringing machine so I could string my own rackets. I estimated that it would take nearly nine months to save enough money to cover the cost of the $1,000 machine.

My first year with the machine was a year of learning to string my rackets quickly—no easy task for an impatient, less-than-handy kid like me. But I worked hard and got my stringing time down. Having recouped my parents' initial investment, it was time to expand. I began stringing for others on my high school team. Surprisingly, even though I charged nearly 30% less than professional stringers, not everyone wanted me to string for them. Still, the string jobs began piling up, and soon there wasn't enough time to play tennis, study and string all in the same day. I gave up studying. My stringing became quicker and I took shortcuts to increase my profits. The holes in several rackets were too small for me to thread the string through easily, so I used a drill to make them a little larger. This cut my stringing time down considerably and no one seemed to mind. Of course, I didn't bother to think about what this drilling might mean for the frame's integrity, but then again, I was committed to the goal of keeping my profit margins as high as possible.

My goal all throughout high school was to get accepted into an Ivy League college. While my grades were important, my athletic achievements would most likely be the determining factor for me. So, building on my nearly 10 years of tennis experience, I began commuting daily to the area's two most premier tennis clubs, both of which were in Trumbull, Connecticut. Players came from all over to train with the top coaches and facilities the Northeast had to offer. After a few marquee high school tennis players began practicing there, the rest of us piled on so we could all push each other to get better. Our state was still far behind the true high school tennis elite of those in Florida and California, but most of us still had a good chance at playing college tennis.

In time, my game got better and better. I was obsessed with winning and trained hard. My stringing business suffered and I did the minimum in school to maintain my grades. Tennis consumed my life. My high school teammates loved my wins but were put off by my intensity. As a result, I didn't get elected captain in my senior season—probably because my teammates knew I'd work them as hard as I worked myself. Focus on the goal and go for it at all costs. That was my motto. My teammates were right to be scared.

I refined my game by perfecting an array of cheap but strategic shots. I was never in good enough shape to truly compete in the world of championship high school tennis. Scrapping was my best chance at winning, so I was determined to become the best scrapper possible. Every now and then my trick shots and dedication would surprise some of the great local players, but I was ultimately no match for them in terms of power and speed. Luckily, they were all seniors and due to graduate soon. This opened up an opportunity for me.

Going into my senior year, our local paper even published an article that said I was considered the top player in the state by default because everybody else had graduated! In the previous year, I lost in the finals of the Class L State High School Championship in a heartbreaking third-set tiebreaker. This loss fueled a great desire in me to win at all costs during my senior year and I ratcheted up my training routine even further. I changed my diet to the perfect mix of protein and healthy carbohydrates and extended my daily practice sessions. I even added an extra cardio and weight-lifting workout after tennis practice each day. I was on a mission. All I could think about was winning the state title. Unfortunately, I'd already planted the seeds to my downfall when I drilled holes into my rackets to save time stringing.

During my senior year of high school, just before tennis season began in the spring, I developed a sharp pain in my elbow that pretty much put an end to my tennis career. I didn't think much of it when it first began, and I got used to playing with pain. But this pain simply wouldn't go away—even after days of rest. I tried every possible remedy from acupuncture and ultrasound treatments to rigorous physical therapy. My family went so far as to drive me into New York City to see a highly reputable specialist. The tests were conclusive; I had almost no cartilage left in my elbow. I was told to rest as much as possible before tennis season and that afterward, I needed surgery. This news was heartbreaking. For several months, I rested, but my elbow pain barely subsided. For the majority of the season, my elbow pain forced me to serve underhand. I lost early in the state championship.

Drilling holes into my rackets to string faster helped me in the short run, but hurt me in the long run. I'm no medical expert, but it seems likely those holes cracked my racket frames enough to be partially or even fully responsible for my injury. If true, then this was just the first of many variables that have shaped the pattern of my life. Working hard and staying focused were the keys to my short-term success, but in the long run, my obsession with winning led me to take shortcuts that undercut any possibility for long-term success.

Despite my lackluster tournament performance, I still managed to basically reach my goal of being accepted into a solid, if not Ivy League, college. Tufts University, a common backup school for many Ivy League candidates, accepted me early, thus rewarding my many years of hard work. Early acceptance into college was particularly satisfying for me because it meant that I could basically stop studying altogether. Tufts would still check my grades, but the pressure to perform was lifted almost entirely. Without tennis and schoolwork in my life, I was free to do whatever I pleased. I now had a great deal of spare time to focus on another longtime passion of mine: the stock market.

Chapter 2: Bitten by the Bug

I first became interested in the stock market when I was 12 years old, but it had always taken a backseat to my tennis career. My first few stocks were in well-known companies: Viacom, the media conglomerate, the Boston Celtics and Supercuts. I chose Supercuts myself as I had some newfound money, thanks to the maturation of the many Series EE bonds that I'd accumulated over the years, while Viacom and the Boston Celtics were gifts from family members.

I began tracking the daily prices of these three stocks in our local newspaper and thought I noticed patterns relating to how their stock prices moved over time. I convinced my parents to allow me to invest $300 in an oil stock whose price action indicated higher stock prices ahead. I invested, but within a few months, the company's stock price had plunged by nearly two-thirds. I was mad that I'd been so stupid and vowed to never speculate again. That would obviously change, but at the time, I was appropriately conservative. I was particularly pleased with my Supercuts investment because they sent their shareholders a quarterly coupon for a free haircut. The free haircuts alone were worth a 20% annual return to me, but when Supercuts was acquired by Regis shortly thereafter, the free coupons ceased, and I sold the stock for a solid gain.

On Supercuts, I made what I thought was a great deal of easy money without really doing anything other than holding the stock for a few months. I loved how that worked and I wanted to learn more about it. My father was a financial planner, so I devoured the finance books from his library, determined to learn about the industry as quickly as possible. His books about the mutual fund industry intrigued me the most because it appeared as though mutual fund managers could earn millions of dollars per year if their investments performed well. This would surely be my profession—or so I told everybody at school.

Nobody had heard of this profession before, so everyone thought me rather strange. I took comfort in knowing that they hadn't done the research I had. Let them study for decades to eventually become lower-paid doctors and lawyers. I knew where the real money was. Nightly, I began watching CNBC—the main television network devoted to finance—to make better sense of the financial world. One night, I even called in to ask a question about AT&T, and, surprisingly, my question was answered on live television. It was the highlight of my life then.

I thought about how fund managers were frequent guests, so if I worked hard enough, I might get the opportunity to be on CNBC, too! Over the next decade, the channel became not only my entertainment of choice but also a key factor in developing what would become my profession.

As a result of my early acceptance to college and hiatus from tennis, I could finally put all my time into online stock trading. Along with my profits from Supercuts, I had $12,000 from bar mitzvah gifts that was wasting away in a savings account. At the time, the stock market was the most popular topic of the day. We were in an incredibly bullish market environment, defying all the skeptics by moving higher and breaking all kinds of records. My parents allowed me to play with my entire net worth, since they thought I'd lose it all rather quickly and that the loss would teach me about the value of a dollar. So, I opened an account with Suretrade, which was by far the cheapest of any reputable online discount brokerage at the time. Suretrade was one of several online discount brokerages that had recently revolutionized the brokerage industry with low commissions of only $10 per stock trade. Previously, big brokerages had charged $50 to $100 for small orders, making frequent trading too costly for small accounts like mine. With these lower commissions, I figured I could learn by trading often, and I'd be protected from paying my broker too much during my education. I was still too young to have my own account, so I opened a custodial account under my mother's name.

I still possessed little market knowledge, but my relative ignorance only fed my desire to accelerate my education. I stopped hanging out with my friends and stayed up late to watch CNBC, review stock message boards, skim through financial websites and read as much financial news as possible. To keep better track of all the different companies, I started writing everything down on note cards. But my home computer was too slow to keep up with my insatiable need for more research.

At school, I began lying to my teachers to get bathroom breaks during classes so I could sneak into the library to do extra research. The school library had the fastest Internet connection around, so it was the perfect place to check all the finance message boards and intraday stock quotes. When my teachers got suspicious of my 20-minute-plus bathroom breaks, I just skipped class altogether. Eventually, my research obsession led me to skip nearly every class and spend entire school days in the library. My absences piled up and the principal was forced to call my parents. My parents were dismayed but let it slide as a kind of reward for my early acceptance into a good college.

Within a few weeks, I'd become good friends with the midday librarian, a curmudgeon Bob Newhart look-alike. We shared a common interest in the stock market, so we debated for hours. He respected me for my unwavering desire to learn, and I respected him for not telling anyone about my skipping class. Even though we disagreed on just about everything, we became fast friends. He was a buy-and-hold investor, while I definitely was not. He constantly tried talking me out of my day trader ambitions, but he eventually consented when he saw that his arguments were falling on deaf ears. He was known around school as a stern old man to be feared, so I gained some notoriety when I jokingly talked down to him in front of other students. I was glad that he allowed me to spend my days freely exploring the Web, and he was glad to have somebody to talk to about the markets. He even went so far as to lie on my behalf.

One time, he told a teacher who was holding class in the computer lab that I desperately needed a computer for an urgent project, even though he knew I'd only use it for market research. She bought his story and kicked a student off his computer, making him share with a classmate. While trying to contain my laughter, I obligingly sat down and got to work.

The incredible amount of time I spent on research allowed me to grasp that there was a full-fledged mania in the then-current market environment. There was so much information and so many varying opinions to absorb; I quickly lost myself in this new digital world.

At the time, I thought I was connected by high-speed Internet, but it was actually incredibly slow compared with today's standards. Today we're used to zipping around the Web, but back then, even the finest computers with the fastest internet connections took at least 10 seconds to load each webpage. So, if you took the time to pull up an article, you'd better read it in its entirety or else it'd just be a waste of time. My nightly research on our home computer was even slower because we had an outdated computer and we used the cheapest Internet service provider. I begged my parents to get America Online because, while more expensive, AOL's online service hosted a message board called "The Shark Tank," where hundreds of traders debated the hottest stocks. Increasingly curious about the Internet, my parents eventually consented, and I was finally able to scroll leisurely through the message board posts without fear of getting detention. The other traders became my first teachers as to the inner workings of the markets.

By November 1998, I was ready to start putting all the research I'd done and my $12,400 to good use. My account had been dormant for nearly a month, but now I bought positions in three *microcaps*, or publicly-traded companies valued under $250 million, whose products seemed as promising as their uptrending stock prices. Unfortunately, I made the same mistake as most first-time traders by checking the stocks so frequently that it seemed like their stock prices barely ever moved. Impatient, I sold them for small losses and decided to focus on Internet stocks because I liked that their stock prices seemed to be able to increase much more rapidly.

At that time, there was an insatiable demand for technology stocks, but nobody knew how long the pandemonium would last. My goal would be to make as much money as possible before the party ended. Long-term investing didn't appeal to me; I just didn't have the patience. Even though I wanted to trade the hottest names alongside most of the other traders I followed, I was forced to trade penny stocks because the hottest Internet stocks of the day—Akamai, Yahoo! and Netscape—were all too expensive for my wimpy little account.

Penny stocks, or stocks priced below $5 per share, represented the only market segment in which I could afford to play, so it wasn't a very difficult choice. I still had little concept of what my $12,400 was really worth, because my years of focusing on tennis had left me ignorant about the costs of living in the real world. After all, I'd never bought anything with my own money other than baseball cards and string for my tennis rackets. I unwittingly took the attitude of Bob Dylan in thinking "When you got nothing, you got nothing to lose" and chose to think of my $12,400 as play money.

I wasn't irresponsible, so I didn't enjoy taking great risks, but after watching the action in the penny stock market from the sidelines for a few weeks, I concluded it was possible to predict with relative precision how stocks would perform in the short term. No, I wasn't a stock picking genius from the start; in those days it wasn't very difficult to recognize that a company armed with a few press releases and an uptrending stock price could surge rather predictably for hours, days and even weeks at a time. Even though the uptrending stock price said buy and hold for as long as possible, I was still too skeptical to be able to hold that long. But I could be tempted to hold for a few hours or days if my gains were large enough. Luckily, I didn't know about short selling at that time and honestly believed the only way to make money in the stock market was to buy stocks low and sell them high.

I was about to discover I was in the perfect place with the perfect naïveté at the perfect time in stock market history. The Dow and the NASDAQ were coming off large drops in the summertime, and the stage was set for a rebound and maybe more. Internet and technology plays were the hottest sectors and drove the market rebound in the winter on its way to a yearlong, record-shattering stratospheric breakout. In layman's terms, the stage was set for me to shine.

Chapter 3: Show Time

My penny stock trading journey began with the recognition
that certain types of company news were the main factors behind
rising stock prices. Positive earnings, product announcements
and partnerships were all the best forms of news. To capture the
greatest gains, the key was to buy as quickly as possible after any
important news was released, but since everyone had access to the
same headlines, the competition was fierce. I knew I could never
compete with the more seasoned professionals in terms of speed,
but it seemed like immediacy wasn't required since the buying
didn't subside for hours and sometimes even days.

Believing I could keep track of all the hottest stocks, I checked the message boards as frequently as possible. I watched and learned as traders' message board posts detailed several different stocks; but after a few days, I saw many of the stocks mentioned had failed to move in the direction their posts had suggested, and many even moved in the opposite direction. Clearly, posters weren't always interested in discussing the hottest stocks; they simply wanted to promote the stocks in which they had positions.

It seems obvious now, but back then I didn't know how to sort through trader chatter. I learned to never again trust message board posts. While I respected these traders' influence, I'd always remember to view posts with a cynical eye. Instead, I turned to the newswires for my trade ideas. Of course, I continued watching CNBC religiously to hone my market knowledge, but the channel focused mainly on the largest, most popular stocks of the day—definitely not the kinds of stocks I was playing.

I gradually mastered the art of scrolling through the websites of the two main newswires to read every press release imaginable and observe the corresponding price action in the stocks. I used three computers at one time so I could designate one computer for each newswire and the third for trading. This setup was sometimes complicated by the fact that the computers in the school library were constantly in use by others. Since finding three computers in a row was usually impossible, I'd reserve three computers at various stations around the room and race like a madman from computer to computer to check and reload the webpages on each computer. The other kids thought I was nuts, but my friend the librarian knew exactly what I was doing. I must've scanned thousands of articles each day. After a few weeks, my eyes were red and sore, but I thought I perceived a definite pattern of how certain press releases helped move stock prices higher.

In those wild times, the truth was that almost any press release helped promote tiny companies. When I say tiny, I mean any company valued under $100 million. Yes, a $50-million company was considered puny; welcome to Wall Street. But penny stocks always responded better when there was a large company mentioned in the press release and better yet when the large company's ticker symbol was included with the release. The practice of including the ticker symbols of large companies in tiny companies' press releases is called *ticker spam*. While the actual news would often be meaningless for the large company, the tiny company would receive substantial recognition thanks to the thousands of investors who tracked the large company's news on a daily basis. Tiny companies lined up to "partner" with large companies like Microsoft, Netscape and IBM in order to reap the benefits of appearing under the news headlines of these well-known giants.

The way it worked was that tiny companies signed up to the partner programs of large companies, even though the two companies wouldn't be working closely together. For a few thousand dollars, almost anybody could sign up to these programs, so it didn't mean anything whatsoever in a business sense. Yet the publicity from such "partnerships" could push a tiny company's market value higher by tens or even hundreds of millions of dollars. Tiny companies sometimes even issued press releases detailing how they intended to use a large company's services. For example, a handful of companies thought it newsworthy to announce that they had become members of AOL's Internet service. So, they used AOL's ticker symbol in the corresponding press release. Remember how thrilled I was when my parents allowed me to have AOL? If I'd been a penny stock, I would've issued a press release to mark the occasion and this information would've boosted my stock price exponentially. Ridiculous, I know. Other companies announced when they designated FedEx as their official shipper. Naturally, a press release using FedEx's ticker symbol was quickly disseminated. These tiny companies understood the marketplace lacked reason, and the smart ones took advantage of it.

After any press release, traders knew they needed to buy as many shares of these tiny companies as quickly as possible because there was no telling how long the publicity would continue to lure buyers. The average daily trading volume for the majority of these companies before any news release amounted to only a few thousand shares, so it wasn't very difficult for their stock prices to rise dramatically on any increased buying. Buying onslaughts of hundreds of thousands or even millions of shares could hit these largely dormant stocks, and only then would the fun really begin.

Sometimes these tiny companies actually signed meaningful deals, in which case somebody from the large company would be quoted in the press release, but more often than not, the deals were largely trivial. It didn't matter to me whether the partnership was significant or not because I knew that many tiny companies used loopholes like these to boost their stock prices. I had no problem buying into companies with meaningless or exaggerated deals, as long as there were other buyers out there driving the stock price higher after me. I was usually able to sell my shares for a small profit before the news was discovered as inconsequential, causing the stock price to drop. At the time, I was as gullible as the next guy and didn't fully understand the way the system worked, so I couldn't hold very long anyway. My impatience worked to my advantage in that fast-paced market.

Back then, popular websites like Yahoo! Finance and PR Newswire gave these tiny companies easy publicity. Today, major news organizations have since adjusted their policies to bar such press releases from appearing under the headlines of large companies. Of course, this revised policy unintentionally hurts tiny companies that do sign meaningful deals with large companies, but no system is perfect.

Another ingenious publicity strategy for these tiny companies was their issuing of press releases stating they had added ".com" to their corporate name. Since technology companies were all the rage, everybody wanted to be one. This superficial change led investors to believe that companies that added a ".com" to their name were on the cutting edge, ready to take advantage of the new age by doing business on the fast-growing Internet. Should the market value of these companies not therefore increase to better reflect their new focus on growth? What a joke! It's amazing how this tactic was successfully used time and again to inflate companies' stock prices. Some companies actually started new, Web-based businesses, while others simply hired some computer nerds to create basic informational websites, most of which didn't even include e-commerce functionality. The actual business execution was irrelevant. Traders didn't care about the business fundamentals of these companies; their only concern was with the companies' ability to issue press releases that would influence other traders to bid the stock price higher. Everyone seemed to be making money from these patterns, including fledgling day traders like me.

It was almost too easy to profit from the effects of these name-change press releases. They were definitely the easiest to spot among the many press releases on the newswires. Within a day, stock prices could rise by 30% or more on these "news items" and could double if a company included a quote from management discussing their new Internet strategies in any detail. If the quote was longer than three sentences, the value of the press release would diminish, since the details would give away the fact that the company's Internet strategy had only limited potential. Their stock price performed better when the company was armed with a press release containing one or two general sentences proclaiming how excited they were about doing business on the Internet. One sentence was actually the best because it showed investors that this company meant business, and yet it was vague enough to allow investors to imagine that they had discovered a future Internet powerhouse.

In the first few months of 1999, I took full advantage of these publicity plays dozens of times—so much so that after three months my account had doubled to $25,000. My average position of 3,000 shares was minuscule in the overall scheme of things in which hundreds of thousands or even millions of shares traded daily. I routinely bet a good portion and sometimes even my entire net worth in one or two companies because the trades proved profitable nearly every time. It was incredibly enjoyable to watch because the stock price increases were steady throughout the day, so I was never really scared to hold my position. The common midday sell-off pattern that made trading larger companies so difficult didn't seem to apply to my penny stocks. When the trading volume and stock price didn't perk up as quickly as expected, I sold my shares. It didn't matter if I had a loss or a gain on the trade; I had to free up my capital to buy stocks that were moving, since there was always another stock to play.

Unfortunately, I didn't have enough money in my account to play everything all the time, and many great plays slipped through my fingers. Still, I rarely held for more than a day after the news got cold or was discovered to be an exaggeration of the truth. Of course, the stock prices didn't seem to care about business reality as they just kept heading higher.

Even though I profited on almost every trade, I consistently sold my shares too early because my nervousness overpowered the bullishness of the uptrending stock prices. Looking back, I consistently sold out when the stock price had risen about 20%. Anything larger would've pushed the investment out of my comfort zone. This tactic makes sense because as greedy as I was, I wasn't foolish enough to risk my overall gains. My success was all happening too quickly for a complete amateur like me. I didn't want to push my luck.

The price surges in these microcap stocks were unprecedented. The stocks somehow held onto daily gains of 30% or more no matter what the overall market was doing. The overall market was volatile and often down a great deal, and yet these publicity plays still held strong. I checked the stocks days after the publicity and trading volume had worn off; surprisingly, their prices still hadn't fallen much. The lack of any meaningful sell-offs gave me a false sense of security even though reason kept me cautious.

After all my quick success, I was surprised to see a general lack of interest in the tiny companies I'd played so effectively. Everyone focused on the much larger Internet plays whose price action seemed to be much less predictable and from which nobody seemed to be able to make consistent profits. CNBC and the message boards focused on when the stock prices of the technology companies with little to no business fundamentals would come crashing back to earth.

In this incredibly bullish market environment, the pessimists were largely outnumbered. Everyone agreed that it was a new world and that the Internet would revolutionize everything. The bullish traders argued that the technology companies' business fundamentals would catch up to their soaring stock prices in time because their businesses were booming.

I didn't take part in what I considered to be a useless debate. I preferred to take advantage of the current market environment rather than worry about any potential widespread change. While the debate was educational, it didn't really matter to me, since my short holding periods insulated me from overall market risk. Plays just kept popping up every day and I kept making money. In my mind, it was rather simple: penny stocks were more predictable than the larger, higher-profile stocks. Of course, there wasn't as much money to be made in my tiny niche, but there was still more than enough for me.

My consistent gains finally allowed me to qualify for *margin*, or the ability to borrow capital from my broker to take positions, so for the first time I could afford to play higher priced stocks. But after much thought, I decided to forgo using margin for the time being and to stick with my tiny niche that had been the source of all my earnings. I reasoned that if popular technology companies without any business fundamentals deserved inflated stock prices based on hype, penny stocks without any business fundamentals likewise deserved inflated stock prices based on hype. Further, penny stocks should experience larger percentage gains due to their lower-priced stocks, so the opportunity for larger profits was much greater.

To this day, I cannot believe I had the insight to understand this, as this line of thinking was definitely the smartest idea I've ever had. My impatience taught me to take large positions and aim for small price moves rather than to take small positions and have to wait for large price moves. Even though I had little market knowledge and even less trading experience, I wisely decided to stay with the niche that I knew and I continued to play it in the way in which I was most comfortable.

In the spring of 1999, after several months of successful short-term trading, I stumbled upon an Internet play that I wanted to hold longer than a few days. It didn't have any special news or trading volume, but their business prospects seemed so bright that I felt compelled to buy into their story. A few months back, WelcomeToSearch Engine, Inc. (WKWG), whose stock traded at $5 per share, had acquired an Internet search engine company and was gearing up to debut their "groundbreaking" product in the next few weeks. I noticed a stunning similarity to a larger Internet search engine company whose stock price had surged from $6 to $30 in the weeks leading up to their product's debut. I wanted to bet this tiny company's stock price would follow suit. This was my chance to both invest for once and also work on my impatience.

I became obsessed with this play and watched almost every trade. I put together spreadsheets of every possible variable, comparing this tiny company with their larger counterpart. I scoured the Internet for everything I could find about WKWG and their industry. Everything reeked of excitement, but their stock lay mysteriously dormant. The lack of action aside, I became convinced that WKWG's stock price could increase exponentially within days once the official press release about their new Internet search engine hit the wires. Contrary to my usual trading strategy, no matter how hard I tried, I knew I couldn't wait for the news to hit before investing. I figured I could take an easy 20 to 30% gain if the news hit afterward, so I pulled the trigger early and bought the stock.

I played it safe by putting only half my net worth into this play, since it wasn't my typical kind of trade. After all, there hadn't been any publicity, trading volume or price movement yet. I wanted others to see what I'd discovered, so I posted my thoughts on multiple message boards. I wanted to demonstrate my market wisdom to everyone and hopefully gain a following if proved correct. My posts would probably also help WKWG's stock price rise if they influenced other traders to place buy orders of their own.

The next day, WKWG followed the pattern perfectly by issuing a press release touting their upcoming product debut. While I congratulated myself on being right, my heart sank as the stock price didn't budge. Both the stock price and trading volume failed to increase like I'd hoped, so I quickly reviewed all my reasons for being invested. The situation's similarity to the large Internet company was uncanny, but maybe the marketplace had matured, rendering this pattern obsolete. Should I sell some of or even my entire position to protect myself from a potentially large loss? I

didn't know what to do. It was maddening. Finally, I decided
to sell some of my shares because it was too risky to stay fully
invested, especially considering the size of my position in relation
to my total capital. After another day of further deliberation, the
stock price dipped a little and I sucked it up, selling my remaining shares for a $1,000 loss.

While the dollar loss wasn't great, I felt completely dejected
because I'd never been surer of anything in my life. I had put
more time into this play than all my previous plays combined,
yet my hard work hadn't gotten me anywhere. I needed to face
reality: I was just a high school senior gambling in a marketplace
I barely understood. Maybe I should stick to my publicity plays
and leave the research to real financial professionals.

Over the next few days, I tried getting back into my normal trading groove, but now even my publicity plays had stopped
working. I was forced to take several more thousand-dollar
losses, and my gloom turned into full-blown misery. And then,
to top it all off, I began receiving nasty e-mails and message
board comments regarding my WKWG posts. I'd obviously been
wrong in my thinking, so other traders felt it their duty to rub it
in. I couldn't blame them—I loved doing the exact same thing
when somebody else was wrong. But I didn't need this right now.
Was this new hobby of mine already at an end? Maybe I was just
overreacting. After all, it was just a small loss. As I continued to
sort out everything in my head, something incredible happened.

WKWG began uptrending on substantial trading volume
but without any news. It was happening just as I'd predicted.
How could this stock move higher without me! I immediately

bought back in by using 75% of my $30,000 account because the stock price and trading volume now confirmed the pattern. I'd been completely correct in my thinking, but I hadn't waited for the price action to confirm that thinking. I'd tried to cheat the pattern by getting in early, and instead, the market taught me a valuable lesson: you can't cheat the market; you can only cheat yourself. After all, you can never know exactly how a stock price will move; every trade is an educated guess. I simply needed to stay disciplined and stick to my trading rules to wait for the variables to align before entering any position.

I quickly raced to post on as many message boards as possible so everyone could now see this pattern, too. I e-mailed everyone who'd bad-mouthed me so they'd apologize or at least take another look at WKWG. Nobody apologized, but some e-mailed me back to say they had now bought a few shares for themselves. Over the next few days, others began echoing my thoughts on various message boards, and the stock price continued to uptrend on hundreds of thousands of shares traded.

But the stock's uptrend wasn't as great or as steady as I'd expected. The many intraday dips concerned me. While the stock price still climbed, it wasn't keeping up with my projections. When the stock failed to break a key price level, I sold my shares, even though the trading volume had increased nicely. In three days, I had ridden the stock for a 17% gain, earning over $4,000 in the process. It was my single greatest profit yet. This trade became my greatest success not only because of the large dollar gain but also because it gave me the confidence from which everything else followed. I might've entered too soon, but I chalked that up to excitement and lack of discipline. More importantly, I went in with a plan, correctly took a small loss when the stock price failed to act as expected, and jumped right back in when the price action better concurred with my thesis. WKWG never moved much higher, and their product subsequently bombed, but it served as a valuable lesson nonetheless: if enough people are willing to buy into a potential pattern, it becomes a self-fulfilling prophecy.

Immediately after my WKWG experience, I took several days off. I used the opportunity to catch my breath and reflect on everything that was happening to me. Was I prepared for the roller coaster ride of playing the stock market? Was I destined to do this for a living? How much money could I actually make if I did? Granted, I hadn't made much yet, but my skills and market knowledge were growing every day. My recent success made me stronger, savvier and more confident in my future. I decided I'd trade as long as these opportunities lasted. Maybe the mania would end soon and I'd be just like any other college-bound student. Hopefully not—this was too much fun!

I began researching other tiny Internet companies with exciting products but dormant stocks. I was finally able to fully devote my time to research and trading, since what little schoolwork I had was now winding down. It took me a few weeks to cut through all the market noise, but I finally discovered two seemingly undervalued Internet plays. This time around, I decided to wait for news before buying, as I was determined to be more disciplined and less impulsive with respect to my trading.

My initial thousand-dollar loss on WKWG proved to be an invaluable lesson because anytime I thought about entering a new play, I was reminded that patience was crucial to my success. There was no point in trying to buy at the exact start of a run; experience had taught me that my lack of patience would make me sell for a loss if the stock price didn't move immediately. I'd never be able to hold for the entire price move, so before buying, I needed to wait for the move to begin, hopping on and off somewhere in between.

My research paid off. My first find was Nettaxi (NTXY), which, at the time, was one of the most popular websites in the world. Surprisingly, their stock languished in the low teens, while less-popular but more vocal Internet companies surged many times over. My other find was Isleuth.com (SLEU), another Internet search engine company in a similar vein to WKWG. Considering my previous success, I bought into their story rather easily.

NTXY was first up when their stock price and trading volume increased, even though there didn't appear to be any news. I put half my account into this new play because it seemed that the most popular Internet-related stocks were surging higher in unison. I aimed to hold my position as long as possible because I knew the company and their popularity were real. Other popular Internet companies were trading at values 7 and even 12 times that of NTXY, so I knew this valuation gap would interest many traders, and I made sure to point that out in all my message board posts. Most posts were aimed at inspiring other traders to add NTXY to their watch list if not buy into it directly. After riding NTXY for a week and making almost 43% on my investment, I couldn't stand it any longer. I needed to sell my shares and turn my paper profits into cold hard cash. The $4,000 profit from WKWG paled in comparison to this trade, as my position in NTXY yielded over $7,000 in profits. My account assets neared $40,000, and as excited as this made me, my newfound wealth scared me more than ever. This was more money than I'd ever seen before; it was no longer just some fun little game. Later, I discovered my parents had even discussed shutting down my account to protect me from my greed but eventually decided to allow me to keep trading and learning. We all agreed that this newfound wealth could go in a heartbeat if I wasn't careful. Such thinking helped me become more conservative than ever.

One week later, the latest Internet search engine play, SLEU, began experiencing the pattern of elevated price action and trading volume in the exact same manner as WKWG and NTXY had. I excitedly hopped on board this new play and waited to collect my prize. In a move that reflected my newfound conservatism, I invested only one-third of my total account. I realized the game had changed because I was no longer aiming for quick profits. Now my profit goals increased along with my fear of taking larger losses. After a few sleepless nights thinking about how this play might be the one to finally sink me, I couldn't hold any longer. After four days, I sold, capturing a $5,000 gain in the process. For weeks afterward, I didn't bother to check the stock price for fear that I'd be tempted to buy back in if it kept rising.

Even with my cautious approach, the emotional rush I felt from trading was a prime motivation for me to push ahead. Profits simply reinforced my commitment. Somehow, it all seemed too easy. Despite my dedication to thorough research, I was concerned about taking such large positions relative to my total assets—all based on my pattern recognition abilities. I'd become somewhat accustomed to large gains because the profits from my last three trades alone equaled the total value of my original account. When would this joyride end?

I continued with this strategy of buying undiscovered Internet companies when their stock prices and trading volume perked up, but like most market-driven trading models, it soon outlived its effectiveness. The main reason for my earlier success had been due to the price action of the larger technology plays. On several occasions, their intraday stock prices climbed by $20 and sometimes even $30 per share, which made these lower-priced technology plays appear extremely cheap in comparison. But during the summer, the buying interest in the larger technology plays diminished and their stock prices fell flat. Now, sometimes they even dropped by $10 to $20 per share intraday.

By the end of the summer, I had traded nearly three dozen tiny technology companies, and yet my account remained stagnant. I profited on a handful of plays, but I found myself betting less each time and getting scared into taking several small losses. For the time being, my strategy stopped working, but I was somewhat relieved to see the market take a breath.

I returned to playing my penny stock publicity plays because the holding periods were short and the trading gains, while smaller, were more predictable. I needed to get back to my comfort zone, so returning to my bread-and-butter strategy, I began putting only one-eighth of my total account—and sometimes even less—into each play. After nine months of wildly profitable trading, I'd become incredibly scared of any potential large losses. After all, I had still yet to take a loss greater than $2,000.

During this time, I took many small gains and losses while trying to get a sense of the marketplace. In time, I believed my profits would increase, but for now I needed patience. In the meantime, I planned to read as much as possible to better understand the markets in general. All of these easy gains made me more determined than ever to gain enough market knowledge to test out more-complex trading strategies that might be more challenging and eventually lead to greater profits.

But it was time to get ready for Tufts. It's ironic that something for which I'd worked my entire life now seemed so irrelevant. At this point, I'd found my calling, and college seemed little more than a distraction. My parents laughed at me when I explained this to them. They advised me to tone down my trading, at least for a while, to get better acclimated to college life. After all, in the grand scheme of things, college was much more important than this small-time day-trading hobby of mine. They had very high expectations of me. I begrudgingly agreed to stop trading for a while, but the market had other plans for me.

Chapter 4: The Freshman 107,000

I hated Tufts University from the start.

The weather seemed colder than Connecticut's. The girls were not to my liking. I'd made a small group of good friends, but they all joined fraternities almost immediately. I thought about joining one, but I knew I wouldn't make it through the hazing, and even if I did, I couldn't keep up with their drinking. My classes were difficult, and I had to work hard to get good grades.

But the worst of it was my housing situation. I guess being an only child I was used to having my own space. Lots of it. I'd drawn a forced triple, which meant that I shared a room with two roommates instead of just one. The room was barely meant for two people, let alone three, so it was extremely tight and crowded. Early on, I banded together with one of my roommates whom I liked, and we planned to irritate the third roommate, who was a local, into leaving. We toyed with him on a daily basis by playing petty pranks on him such as subscribing his e-mail address to pornographic websites and spraying his sheets and pillows with Windex. After a few weeks, our operation succeeded and he moved out and back in with his parents who lived a few blocks away. C'mon, we weren't that bad—we saved him from paying rent! My roommate and I celebrated our newfound space by throwing a party for the dorm.

The best part of my Tufts experience was the high-speed Internet access in my dorm room, which enabled me to get back to my true calling: online stock trading. No more jumping between computers in the school library or dealing with a slow home Internet connection. Sometimes I'd spend all day in my bathrobe researching and trading. It was great. I ignored the outside world and focused on the digital world. In the fall of 1999, the overall market began heating up and I was ready.

The great demand for nearly every initial public offering (*IPO*), or a company's first offer to sell stock to the public, had always made these plays too expensive for me, but the summer lull allowed some deals to sneak through that were actually affordable. Most of the technology IPOs had previously opened above $40 per share, but during the fall the latest deals were opening in the teens. I decided to use a small part of my now $37,000 account to play these reasonably priced IPOs even though I'd never traded in this volatile but potentially lucrative sector before. After all, it was the first time these companies' stocks were publicly-traded so anything could happen. If necessary, I was willing to risk losing some of my capital to help me better understand the IPO market. Any losses could be considered a kind of tuition for my continuing financial education.

I knew the market prices would move quickly, since the trading volume was much higher than what I was used to, but I believed the lower-priced IPOs would entice smaller traders like me. Theoretically, these small buyers should then push the stock prices higher accordingly.

Specifically, two plays had all the ingredients to be higher-priced Internet stocks, but instead they were priced rather inexpensively. I did a fair amount of research and concluded that these two plays were simply less mature companies than the Internet giants of the day. They both had impressive growth rates and bright prospects, and their low IPO pricing should excite the momentum traders enough to want to buy their stocks.

The first IPO opened in the morning, but I waited for a clean break of the day's highs before buying. In the early afternoon, when the breakout occurred, I jumped in with one-third of my account and waited for other traders to bid the stock price higher. I was right on the money, and the perfect price action occurred with startling speed. Within two hours, I had taken a 30% profit on the trade. It was the quickest $3,000 I had ever made and I wished I had been more aggressive in my buying, since my position was only 800 shares.

The following day, I used the same breakout strategy on another technology IPO. This time it took two incredibly strenuous days with many ups and downs before I reached my target of a 30% gain. The good news was that I was more aggressive this time: I bought 1,200 shares and was rewarded with a $4,300 gain. By the end of the summer, I was surprised how easily my account had broken through its all-time high to reach $44,000. The key was simply waiting for the right opportunities to present themselves. I was happier and cockier than ever.

I tried playing a few more lower-priced IPOs but without the same success. It was amazing how quickly this breakout strategy stopped working. I woke up early every day hoping to find new opportunities, but the worthy plays were few and far between. I tried some riskier plays in which the price action and trading volume weren't particularly extraordinary, but I was forced to take several quick losses. I even held onto plays longer, hoping they might eventually come back so I could break even. Instead, their prices drifted steadily lower and my losses grew in size.

One such play resulted in a $5,000 loss. This was the largest loss I had ever taken. For some reason, I'd been too stubborn to sell and held for a painful two months. That's not a typo; a guy who had difficulty holding stocks for more than two days refused to take a small loss and held a losing position for an entire two months!

I couldn't go back to my publicity plays, because the market had tired of companies using tricks like adding ".com" to their corporate names. Now, only the worst companies were desperate enough to try to use this kind of tactic to push their stock prices higher. By the beginning of November 1999, my account languished near $38,000, and I was incredibly depressed.

I created paper accounts to test different strategies and to get back into my trading groove. Unfortunately, this made me even more hesitant to trade, since each of my imaginary portfolios was solidly in the red. I still continued to trade with real money throughout, but I never risked more than a small fraction

of my total account and I rarely held overnight. This was a time
to categorize, learn and adapt to current market conditions. By
this point, I'd already blown through several different trading
strategies, so I really didn't have any idea if and when I'd ever be
successful again.

I resorted to writing a newsletter dedicated to debating
different stock picks and trading strategies with other traders.
Extremely proud of my past trading success, I began sharing all
of my ideas on various message boards and built a following of
nearly 300 people. I didn't send out ideas very often, but I engaged in many ongoing side conversations with dozens of individual traders. I figured my newsletter could be especially useful
to help me discuss future plays if I ever came up with another
WKWG-type play.

I worked hard to promote and grow my subscriber base by
posting sign-up links on various financial message boards. There
seemed to be new message boards popping up every day now,
but there was no one reliable source for all the information. The
"Shark Tank" on AOL used to be the main destination for interesting message board posts, but it had lost its appeal because too
many beginners now infested the board. There were thousands of
people with inflated accounts who craved further profits. Many
more heard the success stories, and they wanted in, too. Everyone
was trying to gain a better understanding of the marketplace and
find new plays from which to profit.

Nothing in my life really seemed to matter anymore if it
didn't concern the stock market. Tennis, food, friends, school,
girls and material goods all faded into the distance as trading

took center stage. I scoured the Internet and watched CNBC
by day and read finance books and magazines by night. I spent
countless weekends in our school library and checked out business books by the dozen. To substitute my lack of real-world
business experience, I wanted to absorb all their lessons.

Many books were useful and helped my understanding
of the general foundations of the stock market and business in
general. However, their rules definitely didn't apply to this new
fast-paced technology-driven marketplace. Clearly, the markets
were at a crossroads. The old guard had no way of understanding
this new environment, because their years of experience and wisdom only hindered their ability to ride these wild times. In this
pandemonium, lifelong rules ceased to exist. Only potential and
hype mattered, not business fundamentals or the lack thereof.
Only those nimble enough to adapt to the game's new rules could
succeed in this market environment.

There was a general feeling of excitement as the markets
gradually trended higher throughout the year. I wasn't making
much money from trading at the time; I was in regroup mode.
But there was so much information to sort through that I didn't
have time to sit around and mope. I kept track of all the potential strategies in addition to all the plays that could potentially
be worthwhile. My watch lists grew to cover nearly 500 different
companies. It became more and more difficult for me to accu-
rately remember all the statistics of all the various companies.

The Internet had become the best place for all financial
information and the most efficient route for playing the market,
which helped usher in a completely new generation of investors
and traders, including myself. However, more often than not, we

had little to no experience in this industry so we naively accepted the madness surrounding us. Online brokerage commissions had become so cheap that it barely cost us anything to move in and out of positions quickly. News could move stock prices violently within minutes and hours, making the old daily and weekly business publications irrelevant. Message board posts, whether they were factual or just plain hype, moved stocks in real time. News services proliferated as the amount of freely available real-time information mushroomed out of control. For the first time, the information revolution helped thrust little-known companies into the spotlight when they'd never had any outlet to mainstream media before. New plays appeared daily, and they needed to be categorized, investigated and traded quickly in the ongoing quest for trading profits. It was a brave new world.

When I began trading, there had been only a thousand or so daily message board posts, but by this point, I was checking upwards of 10,000 each day. To get a sense of which users to trust, I once read and researched every message thoroughly while keeping notes on index cards. Now, there were just too many to keep track of. I barely had time to skim every new message, since most messages weren't very useful. People posted fake news, and the stocks mentioned would move higher. People posted rumors, and the stocks mentioned would move higher. People reposted press releases, and the stocks mentioned would move higher. Now, any kind of message board mention could influence stock prices! Reality was irrelevant; only fluff mattered; and the more people who believed the fluff, the better a stock performed.

I didn't want to play the fluff game, so I posted only factual information. Lying on message board posts was not only unethical and possibly illegal, it was downright disgusting. Fed up with all this misinformation, I created my own message board to debate and share ideas with a few trusted traders. Our group would be better than the others because we would be honorable and not permit any fluff whatsoever. The posts could contain only publicly available information, thereby making the content more real and interesting compared with the often gossipy posts on other boards. In theory, the accuracy of our posts should help our popularity. Anyone could post, but I'd delete posts I considered to be spam or fluff. Users might even follow the group leaders in trading positions if we could prove our merit through successful market calls.

I'd lead the board at first, but anybody could eventually take the lead as it was an open competition to see who could post the most useful information. It was my hope that our posts might even be able to influence some serious money over time. Yes, I'd just started trading, but I already had big dreams. Many other message boards charged their users for access, but I figured our group's collective buying power would help me earn more in trading rather than the few thousand dollars I could've earned in subscription fees. There was no way to tell how long the current mania would last, so I needed to get as many people on board as quickly as possible. Ideally, we'd all make a little money and help each other discover new plays. I must've been delusional to actually believe that this type of message board would actually last. But I really was that young and naive.

The group was somewhat successful from the start, with a dozen or so traders posting factual descriptions of the stocks in play. Our message board helped everyone involved because we learned from each other while debating different plays in an intelligent manner. It was great to exclude the beginner-type questions and devious posts that were commonplace on other boards. I mixed my message board posts with newsletter recommendations, and after a few weeks of dozens of successful picks, the group surged to 400 members and my newsletter grew to over 600 subscribers. My trading gains resumed as it seemed like new plays kept popping up daily and there was no end in sight. To handle all my watch lists, I began using online software because of the sheer number of stocks in play.

The white-hot market for technology companies had lost any semblance of reason and had turned into a full-fledged mania. In less than two months, the NASDAQ gushed higher by 50% while the Dow only rose 10%. The stock prices of technology-related companies seemed to move only higher without much resistance of any kind, while the stock prices of companies in every other industry remained flat or sank lower. Valuations no longer mattered; all that mattered was whether a company was in play or wasn't. If the momentum crowd was involved, investors made money; if they weren't, investors made nothing. Those who applied reason and talked about overvaluation didn't comprehend this environment. We thought of them as dinosaurs.

Around this time, I noticed the Over-The-Counter Bulletin Board (OTCBB) market was becoming incredibly liquid exceedingly fast. This was an exchange for more developmental companies, since none of them qualified to list on the larger exchanges like the NASDAQ, the American Stock Exchange (AMEX) or the New York Stock Exchange (NYSE). This exchange was created in 1990 but hadn't really taken off until this most recent bull market. Now there was a chance that the increased liquidity and volatility of the overall market might trickle down to offer some quality trading opportunities in this tiny niche. With the market for technology-related companies white-hot, many of the most popular Internet stocks were now trading in the $100 price range. This was much too rich for the blood of most of the newer market players like me. Instead, we turned to this little-known marketplace for tiny companies with lower-priced stocks.

As tiny as some of the companies I'd previously played were, they paled in comparison to the companies listed on the OTCBB. On this exchange, some of the companies filed financial reports with the SEC, but many didn't. Due to the substantial risks involved, some brokerages wouldn't even allow their customers to trade stocks listed here. Until now, these factors combined to limit the liquidity of these plays. Now, many traders didn't mind taking on some additional risk. The 10 most actively traded OTCBB-listed companies used to trade a few hundred thousand shares or a million shares daily, but now their average daily trading volume grew to 2 million and sometimes even 3 million or 4 million shares. The amount of trading volume was now huge, even if the dollar amounts still remained insignificant, since the average stock traded in the 50¢ range. Many of these tiny companies had only a few million shares outstanding, so in a single day, their entire supply of shares could trade many times over if the buying power was great enough. The stocks could similarly surge many times over, since there weren't enough sellers to keep up with the demand without increasing prices substantially.

As much as I hated Tufts, I am forever thankful that I attended the school for three reasons. The first was the high-speed Internet connection, of course. The second and third were the two incredibly influential classes I took: microeconomics and macroeconomics. These two classes helped me understand the theories behind supply and demand at this crucial time. These theories were responsible for nearly all of the subsequent profits I earned from trading hundreds of OTCBB-listed companies.

Since it was a completely new marketplace for me, I began trading OTCBB-listed companies by using only about 10% of my total assets. The order executions weren't as fast because brokers had to call in the orders manually. I could still submit my orders online, but the brokers would have to physically pick up their phones and call in the orders. Yes, that's right, even though we were in the midst of the Internet revolution, the process by which orders were executed in this marketplace was severely behind the times.

I bought into the stocks with the most solidly uptrending prices and planned to hold my shares for a few days. It started out great, with the price increases being very gradual. Amazingly enough, these stocks didn't even require news to be able to move higher. Instead, they just needed trading volume, so I became obsessed with charting each stock's trading volume metrics. Instead of scrolling through thousands of daily press releases, I began scrolling through thousands of daily stock charts and their corresponding trading volumes. To my surprise, I found myself taking 20%-plus gains within a few hours of my buying because the stocks moved very quickly on little trading volume compared with publicity plays. I was definitely back in the game.

These stocks moved so quickly that I found myself hesitant to take large positions because I thought somebody was somehow playing games with me. Couldn't these stocks move lower as quickly as they moved higher? Of course that was a possibility, but they never did. I cursed my need to sell out so early, since these stocks would frequently double or triple in price within days. The reasoning behind my conservatism was that I didn't understand the motivation behind the buying, so I had no way of predicting if and when any potential sell-off might occur. How could these stocks be moving exponentially higher without any news whatsoever? Sure, there were press releases every now and then, but they didn't seem to affect stock prices one way or the other. Who was doing all this buying? I turned to the booming message boards for answers, but all I found was more hype. So, I continued to take small positions because I respected the uptrending stock prices and trading volume increases.

By the beginning of December 1999, my account had easily cleared the $50,000 mark and stood at a mind-blowing $72,000. Daily gains of $2,000 and $3,000 were now the norm. What had I gotten myself into? I didn't have to hold my positions for very long, and the research was minimal. This was great! It was happening quicker than ever, so I didn't even have time to digest this latest round of wealth creation. I wasn't the only confused person, as it was around this time that people truly began flocking to the message boards en masse in search of answers.

My newfound wealth made me feel like a trading pro and I'd almost forgotten my scrappy ways. I now considered trading to be a gentleman's game and I didn't want to see it corrupted by the miscreants who'd somehow gained entrance to our clubhouse. I took immense pride in each dollar I had earned, and I knew that cheating, whether successful or not, was not for me.

I was making money consistently, but my exit points and price targets were almost always off. It was the same old story: I consistently sold too early. The wisest people who read my message board posts probably followed only my *buy* recommendations while ignoring my *sell* recommendations. Still, my posts were the most consistently profitable out of all, so I deservedly became the most respected trader in the group. I received many thankful e-mails and message board posts as people everywhere told me of how they intended to spend their newfound profits. Our group's subscribers were worldwide, although most were U.S. based. They told me stories of how their trading profits were really coming in handy to pay household bills, their children's tuitions and their rent and mortgages.

Some people sent small gifts of appreciation, while some even journeyed to Boston to meet me in person and pick my brain over dinner or coffee. Nobody dared take me to lunch because everyone understood that the daytime was meant for trading and nothing else. I loved seeing the look on people's faces when they came to my dorm room to see that I was really just a college freshman who'd helped them make so much money. I was happy to help because I loved picturing ordinary people being able to solve their financial problems through trading. As the thankful letters and gifts piled in, I thought of myself as a kind of "man of the people." It'd all gone to my head very quickly.

The positions I took got smaller even though my trading frequency increased along with my account size. I now bought only 1,000 or 1,500 shares at a time because my trust in companies and traders, while already scant to begin with, evaporated completely in this circus. My comfort zone gradually allowed for longer holding periods as I rationalized my smaller positions allowed for quicker exits. Under this conservative approach, the consistency of my profits increased even though the dollar gains didn't. I was much more comfortable and enjoyed many more sleep-filled nights when I focused on small gains. While my average dollar gain dropped to approximately $1,000 per trade, the number of plays increased, so through the winter of 1999, my weekly income neared $8,000.

As horrible as I was with my entry and exit points, I was much more comfortable with the size of my current profits amid all the confusion of the marketplace. I would've taken larger positions if I'd better understood the reasons behind the buying, but there were few definitive answers. News wasn't driving these price surges, and the message boards reeked of confusion. The most reasonable explanation was that small investors were buying en masse because they were searching for small, undiscovered technology plays. Not many people could afford the well-known technology companies anymore because those were more expensive than ever. This was the same old story, so I didn't put much stock into it. The surest path to consistent profits appeared to be my current strategy, so I was at peace with my trading style. I closed out the year with several tiny trading losses, but they didn't bother me in the least. I was in a celebratory mood. My account finished the year at nearly $120,000—a gain of nearly $107,000!

Chapter 5: Happy New Year!

I didn't have time to celebrate the new millennium because the trades just kept coming. The NASDAQ continued its run, rising another 25% on top of the 50% it'd already risen over the previous few months. The most popular technology-related stocks were now almost uniformly trading in the $100 to $200 price range, so to the newer traders, the tiny companies I was playing seemed more affordable than ever. Now the trades were coming so fast that I couldn't play all of them and was forced to play only the most promising of the bunch.

I liked watching every single trade so I began skipping my college classes to watch the market action. I wisely enrolled in several night classes to free up enough time to be able to do this. The volatility of the marketplace scared me away from playing many of the largest daily movers, since the tremendous price increases in these stocks had led to increased downside risk. Previously, the stocks with the largest gains barely dropped after their price surges ended, but profit taking now appeared inevitable.

The stocks themselves were more expensive, with the 50¢ and $1 stocks from the winter now trading in the $5 to $10 price range. These $5 to $10 stocks could now move to $20 and even the $40 price range while falling back to the teens or single digits all within a few days. As crazy as it sounds, the intraday price patterns for these companies were rather predictable. The price surges seemed to intensify whenever these stocks broke through round numbers like $10 or $15 per share. Once a stock broke out to new highs, it could run higher by $1 or maybe even $2 per share without any pullbacks whatsoever. This cycle of exponential gains and steep declines quickened, and it seemed likely that the mania would end shortly. But it never did. The plays just kept coming, and I kept trading them.

I rarely played the stocks with the largest daily percentage gains—focusing instead on stocks with medium-size daily gains. The particular companies I played didn't even matter because I played everything; all that mattered were their price patterns. I bought the stocks when their trading volume spiked along with their prices. I loved to watch the persistent sellers try to hold the stock prices down but inevitably get squashed when the buying ramped higher. Those sellers must've been pretty angry because if they had had the patience to hold for a few more hours or days, they would have had gains of 15 to 30%. I was somewhat wiser now, so I held for one or two days longer while the stock prices soared higher.

My percentage gain on each play dropped, but my increased account size allowed me to invest greater dollar amounts, so my overall profits remained steady. My target stocks frequently rose by 10 to 20% daily, but their potential downside was only 5 to 10%. This compared with the largest daily gainers that moved higher by 200 to 300% but that also dropped 40 to 60% intraday when their bottoms fell out. That wasn't the place for me because this new marketplace gave no warning as to when prices would sputter. Stock prices gradually rose for hours, days or weeks at a time and then fell by 50% in a matter of minutes. The potential downside wasn't worth the upside, so I stayed away from that level of play.

My conservatism paid off as I consistently profited while limiting my exposure to potential disasters. After only one month into the new year, my account had surged to $250,000. I almost couldn't believe it; I had just doubled my account and made nearly $130,000 in one month! Oh, how I loved this game. There was no doubt anymore; I was definitely onto something here even if I didn't know exactly how much longer it would last. Amazingly, my losses were still minimal as I rarely lost anything more than $2,000. Comparatively, the gains on some of my trades now topped $10,000. By the beginning of February 2000, I was so confident in my trading that I upped my average position from 1,000 to 5,000 shares. The average daily trading volume in my target stocks swelled into the millions, so my tiny positions made me feel more comfortable than ever.

Even with my success, I was still a very tiny fish in a rather large pond. The good news was that this tiny fish was beginning to make some serious money. Luckily, I didn't have any free time to spend my newfound wealth because trading and schoolwork consumed my entire life. As much as I began craving a few luxury items, I didn't want to take any money out of my accounts because each dollar was being put to good use for trading. I was profiting on 85 to 95% of my trades, and such a profitability ratio was simply unheard of.

Unfortunately, it was around this time that my message board followers stopped sending me gifts. They must've realized that I'd continue posting my picks just to show everyone that I was right. My ego drove me, but I also shared my thoughts because I was pleased that I could help others. I devoted much of my time to the group, and my followers became my closest friends in the digital world. While other people also posted their stock picks, I rarely ever followed anyone else, since my picks were already the most consistently profitable. My superiority complex was quickly spinning out of control—I knew it was—but I accepted it because this overwhelming confidence also helped me take even larger trading positions, which led to greater profits.

I even stopped studying for weeks on end because the time I spent researching my trading strategies and maintaining my group was more important to me than schoolwork. I thought of myself in competition with everyone else on my message board to see who could make the most money, and the results were posted daily. I wouldn't benefit from the lessons of my schoolwork until many years from now. Trading continued to be the number one priority. I didn't want the good times to end.

So many new message boards began popping up around me that I began to lose track. I belonged to nearly 200 different groups, but I joined them only so I could message their members to make them switch their allegiance to my group. I worked harder than ever to get the word out about my personal trading success in order to expand the group and satisfy my ever-growing ego. We were a free group, but we were still tiny compared with many others. I chalked it up to the tiny marketplace in which we dealt because everyone knew the big money simply wasn't there. CNBC had still yet to mention any of the companies we played. But I was successful enough in my efforts that our group grew to over 3,000 members and my newsletter increased to 1,200 subscribers. I now felt like a father, viewing each new group member as my own child who needed nurturing. I was master of my own little domain.

I updated my numbers daily, bragging to everyone about the incredible returns my strategies yielded over various time frames. It didn't matter which time frame I used in my calculations as my gains were all rather absurd. By now, I had made over 1800% in one year and 110% in less than one month. Even though there were many people who doubted my abilities, I was sure to be completely truthful in all my claims. The few nonbelievers faded rather quickly, since I publicly proved my trading abilities day in and day out. I still had no idea why my pattern-based plays were so successful or where all the buying power was coming from, but I continued to trade in a fearless manner nonetheless. I probably should've charged a commission or at least a subscription fee for all my picks, but I was riding high and considered any money I might've made from commissions or fees to be chump change.

When you make the kind of money I was making at such a young age, people talk. Friends, family and even friends of friends all wanted me to help them play the markets on their behalf, and I was only too happy to bring more people into my little trading circle. My roommate and some of my other friends allocated a few thousand dollars to me to trade on their behalf, and I planned to give them a proportionate amount of the profits. I didn't even consider taxes or potential losses.

My popularity on campus was now at an all-time high because many students had heard my story and began spending days in my dorm room to watch me trade. I'd put on shows for my band of disciples, lecturing them about how this niche was better than the rest of the market. I knew that trading without understanding was boring, so my goal was to educate my little fan club through entertainment. Frequently, there were a dozen college students staring at me in awe while they watched me make $10,000 to $30,000 in any one sitting.

One nerdy student in particular, who traded his dad's account, began applying my strategies and was quite successful. He'd found me through a friend of a friend, but he became my most devoted disciple. I never knew how much money he played with, but I noticed the trading volume spike whenever I told him what stock was in play. So I assumed he had a sizable account. My guess is that he made $30,000 or so from my picks over the course of a few weeks. He knew I had a weakness for good food, so he brought me delicacies like caviar and gourmet cheeses and took me out to dinner after each successful trade. I could never remember his name, so I resorted to calling him "Millhouse," after one of the characters on *The Simpsons*. I was cocky and insensitive, and he probably held back from decking me only because he couldn't risk losing my money-making abilities. For better or worse, money—and particularly the ability to make money for others—truly is power.

By this time, I'd noticed that my smaller orders executed much faster than my larger orders. Hmmm, maybe I should open multiple accounts in order to submit several small orders instead of one large order? I had little concept of how my orders were routed, so I decided to test my thinking by opening several accounts. I started two more accounts at Suretrade, since they'd always been good to me. I entered one order of 2,000 shares in each of my two new accounts and one order of 4,000 shares in my original account. Then, I timed how quickly each order was executed. I repeated this process nearly a dozen times, and there was no doubt about it. Lo and behold, when I submitted smaller orders, my execution time improved dramatically, so I submitted the paperwork required to open even more accounts. The difference was just a few seconds on each trade, but in a fast-moving market, that meant thousands of dollars, so it all added up.

Over the next few weeks, I opened two more accounts with another online discount brokerage—E*Trade—and was now trading with five total accounts. Having so many accounts reduced individual orders to 1,000-share lots, so my execution times were much faster. I loved my newfound ability to rapidly get in and out of trades because I was still unsure as to whether my recent gains would hold. The steady stream of daily profits helped keep my confidence high, but I became obsessed with protecting myself from the potential downside of the market's volatility. Could I find a time period during the trading day that might protect me from intraday sell-offs?

My target stocks gained on a daily basis, but this bullish pattern wasn't as gradual on an intraday basis. Intraday price dips frequently tricked me into panicking and scaring me out of my positions before they disappeared, allowing stocks to resume their uptrends. As much as I would've liked to hold through these dips, I was right to sell because these small price drops could've easily turned into large price drops very quickly. It was definitely better to sell early rather than to risk a large price drop later. As frustrating as this was, I was determined to follow my trading rules for safety's sake. While these large price drops occurred less than 5% of the time, my recent gains made me more nervous than ever.

After combing through thousands of stock charts, I thought I'd discovered a pattern that might limit my risk. The pattern called for me to take positions only during a very specific time of the trading day. It was shocking, but the pattern said to buy right before the market close and sell after the market open the next trading day. How could this be? Holding positions overnight went against everything I'd ever learned as a trader. Due to the possibility of overnight news affecting stock prices in any number of different ways, this was the single riskiest time to hold positions.

Upon further research, I was forced to accept this pattern. The daily gainers seemed to rise perfectly before the market close and to *gap higher* into the next morning. After the market open, they frequently surged higher during the first 30 minutes of trading as buy orders streamed in and sellers were overpowered. These price *gaps* in their stock charts may have been minimal—usually only 20¢ to 30¢ per share—but this worked approximately 95% of the time. The statistician in me loved the idea from the start. At this point, I didn't realize that I'd simply stumbled onto a commonly used trading tactic. Instead, I thought I had revolutionized the wheel, or at least that's what I told everyone.

Theoretically, stocks gap higher when positive company or industry news is released after the market close. The news makes buyers unable to wait until the market open the next morning to place their buy orders, so their orders pile up in the pre-market and stock prices subsequently rise, thereby inducing sellers to act to accommodate the many incoming buyers.

OTCBB-listed companies were different in that they never needed news or really even any specific reason to gap higher; the buy orders simply piled up in the mornings for no apparent reason. Their stock prices would rise by 20¢, 30¢ and sometimes even more. Few people wanted to sell at the market open—especially since the stock prices were gradually uptrending—so the gains continued into the late morning. I had no idea why people wanted to buy right at the market open; my best guess was that many people placed their buy orders before they left for work so they'd be assured a position by day's end. I was forced to respect yet another market pattern even though I didn't fully understand it.

Once I discovered this pattern, I began buying these stocks just before the market close and holding overnight. Ideally, the pattern would work its magic and I would sell within the first 30 minutes of the market open the next trading day. While I was nervous about this strategy at first, I gradually became more comfortable. The immediate daily trading gains did much to ease my concerns, so I adopted this new strategy more and more. Having already taken my profits in the morning, I had more time to devote to schoolwork and additional market research. On any given day, there'd be only two or three OTCBB-listed companies

fitting this pattern, so the plays weren't very difficult to spot. I
scanned thousands of charts on other exchanges, but the pattern
seemed to work exclusively in this tiny niche. Very strange, but
I went with it. At first, I bought 500 shares of each gap-up play
in each of my five accounts, but it worked so well that I quickly
scaled my positions to 2,000 shares per account. As I initially
feared, sometimes there was news overnight or before the market
opened, but it didn't matter unless it was truly horrible.

One time I was unlucky enough to be invested in one of
these companies when the news was negative, and I suffered the
greatest loss of my career at that time. The play was Electronic
Identification (EISQ), a developmental technology company
whose stock had risen after issuing a press release announcing
a partnership with Hewlett-Packard for the production of $500
million worth of smart cards. The press release seemed authentic
and brought me back to the days of my publicity plays, but the
company's perfectly uptrending stock price was the main reason
I bought. This news caused the stock price to break out to an
all-time high on tremendous trading volume, so I bought the
standard 10,000 shares divided among my many accounts right
before the market close.

Unfortunately, after the market close, Hewlett-Packard
issued a press release basically refuting EISQ's claims. Damn! I
knew I'd get burned when the stock opened the next day, but the
waiting made it worse—I hardly slept that night. My position
amounted to just over $70,000; how much of that would disap-
pear before I would be able to get out? Maybe the SEC would
halt the stock and it would be months before it reopened—if it
reopened at all. That was unlikely. I knew I needed to get out

immediately so I tried selling everything at the market open, but
a gap-down was inevitable. In pre-market action, sell orders can
pile up just as easily as buy orders, so the market makers adjust
the stock price downward to find the price that will attract buyers to accommodate all these sellers.

My small order sizes helped my quick executions and I sold
within the first 20 minutes after the market open, taking a loss
of just under $30,000. I couldn't imagine who was stupid enough
to buy my shares as EISQ moved continuously lower, finishing
down a staggering 60% on the day. I remember being shocked
that their price didn't fall further, since Hewlett-Packard had
exposed EISQ's press release as misleading. Still, EISQ managed
to bounce over the next few days because the hype hadn't worn
off, but I was done with it.

While the EISQ loss hurt, in the grand scheme of things it
didn't really matter. It was inevitable that I'd get burned eventually. I was just playing the odds in cases like this. Looking back,
I'm surprised that this didn't happen more often, given the companies I traded. I'd already traded hundreds of companies with
questionable attributes, but this was the only time that I'd ever
been burned. No matter, I went right back to work buying before
the market close and selling at the market open the next day.

But returning to trading as if nothing had happened proved
difficult; my nerves were shaken from this recent loss. I reduced
my average position to 5,000 shares on the off chance that the
market had finally matured and was about to beat the stock prices of these tiny companies down to where they most likely belonged. Instead, the demand continued and dozens of OTCBB-
listed companies surged even higher. After two consecutive days

of earning $6,000, my confidence was largely restored and I returned to taking 10,000-share positions. Within one week, my confidence was fully restored as I made back all the money I had lost and more.

By mid-February 2000, my trading had never been better as I had already made nearly $100,000 that month alone. This brought my year-to-date winnings to $230,000. My family accountant said that my incredible earnings meant that I'd have to pay quarterly taxes. I begrudgingly agreed and set aside a rather large chunk of my accounts to pay the Internal Revenue Service (IRS) in April. I became obsessed with my net worth—even though it fluctuated daily—comparing my short-term earnings with the average annual salaries of successful people in nearly every industry. Year-to-date, the only people who seemed on par with me were professional athletes. In fact, my father had a friend who was a golfer on the PGA Tour, so I began comparing his yearly winnings with mine. Through February, I was slightly ahead if only tournament prize money counted, but due to his many endorsement deals, he was probably far ahead of me. I even went so far as researching whether anybody in the finance world had any endorsement deals, but no one did.

As much as I relished the time I spent researching, I maintained my focus on trading because each day truly mattered. I was now averaging nearly $10,000 in daily profits; it was completely out of this world. As I neared my one thousandth career trade, my trading was nearly entirely mechanical. My trading routine helped me tune out most of my nervousness and excitement, keeping me focused on harvesting daily gains from my target stocks. Due to the continued risk, I still ignored the largest daily winners while remaining focused on the second-tier movers. My average position increased to 15,000 shares, which I divided among my five accounts. It had become somewhat complicated to correctly enter the different orders and I sometimes screwed up, losing a few hundred or thousand dollars in the process. Overall, I still considered my system pretty efficient, so the trading days passed with continuous profits and few incidents.

One such trading mishap involved my roommate's girl-friend. Their relationship was on the rocks, so many of their recent conversations had been rather heated. One mid-February night, his girlfriend called repeatedly throughout the night. They'd talk for a few minutes before the conversation ended in some new argument. She called nearly a dozen times from 12 to 4 a.m., so I didn't get much sleep that night. I didn't even have an alarm clock at that time. I always seemed to wake up an hour or so before the market open because I liked getting a head start on the day's research. After my sleepless night, though, I acci-dentally slept until 10:30 a.m., forgetful of the overnight position I held.

Within a few seconds of consciousness, I realized my error and ran to my computer to discover that my overnight position had indeed gapped higher perfectly but had then proceeded to fall by 20% during the next hour. I wasn't very surprised because the stock was in the later stages of its run-up and a fall was inevitable. I sold immediately, but still sustained an $18,000 loss, due to my carelessness and my room-mate's girlfriend. That very afternoon, I purchased two alarm clocks to make sure I'd never get caught in this predicament again. I never completely forgave my roommate's girlfriend for the incident, even though she vowed to pay me back if she ever had $18,000 to spare.

Despite that incident, my roommate and I became closer throughout the year and we began playing the game "How much did Tim make today?" After class, he'd walk into our dorm room and blurt out several guesses. I wouldn't answer until his guess was within a few hundred dollars of the correct answer. It usually took him a minute or two to get close to the answer because my daily profits were all over the place. Once he'd guessed correctly, I liked to launch into speeches, providing all the glorious details of my trades. While I lectured, he'd sometimes nod his head in agreement, but I never knew how much he really understood.

My roommate's reaction was not unique at that time, as nobody seemed to be able to make sense of how I was making so much money. I didn't think it was that complicated, but by now, it was second nature to me. The one thing people did understand was that I was making some serious money, so several friends had asked me to trade their accounts on their behalf. I agreed and within a few months, I had already doubled and tripled their accounts, so everyone was thoroughly impressed.

By the spring of 2000, I was forced to stop trading on behalf of others because it had become too complicated. Now there were too many accounts, calculations and different orders to track while trying to hold on to my sanity. I stopped responding to the dozens of daily e-mails I received, because the allure of easy money had brought too many beginners to my doorstep. I no longer had the patience to deal with their naïveté. I neglected my message board group because I was tired of deleting all the beginner questions and fluff that people were posting. I stopped posting and managing the group because I felt the members had forgotten the reason it existed, allowing the wannabe stock traders and promoters to take control.

My days of helping people were over; now I needed to focus exclusively on myself. This definitely wasn't a little game anymore; I was making real money and I had to protect my assets. I also needed as much time as possible to continue my market research, due to the size of my daily bets, which now exceeded $150,000. Somehow, I kept up with my studies as I enjoyed the challenge they presented me. I think that they put into perspective how surreal my life had become. This realization blurred the line between fantasy and reality, enabling me to take greater risks. Sometimes I wasn't completely sure that the money in my accounts was even real. I stared at the computer screen for hours at a time, trying to soak up what all this newfound wealth really meant. People began treating me differently, and even though I hadn't spent any of my earnings on anything besides my two alarm clocks, I took comfort in my newfound ability to buy whatever I wanted. This was my mind-set when a new company popped onto my watch list.

Chapter 6: Once in a Lifetime

This was the play I'd been waiting for. In early 2000, Illinois Superconductor (ISCO, now ISO)(*t*) announced a revolutionary technology that promised to greatly expand the range of cell phone towers. This was back in the early days of cell phones, so fuzzy connections were commonplace and extremely annoying. The description of ISCO's breakthrough product was detailed and scientific, making the company's prospects very attractive. Their stock price quickly surged from the $1 range in January to the low teens by mid-February. Due to the stock's propensity to gap higher, I had played ISCO a few times, but the daily trading volume had always been too low to ever really interest me.

One Friday morning in late February, ISCO issued a press release stating that over the weekend, their revolutionary technology would be featured on a national news program. The stock's trading volume exploded. The press release even managed to get *me* excited. I figured the publicity would be great, even if the product turned out to be a dud. The stock price had already climbed 25% for the day and nearly 100% for the week, but I knew the hype machine would work overtime during the weekend and the stock would be a perfect gap-up candidate for Monday morning.

At this point, I was already living in a dream world, so why not push my luck? I put nearly three-quarters of my net worth at the time into this play, buying 10,000 shares for about $17 each before the market close. It was a bold bet to say the least. If for some reason the news program dropped the piece or, worse, featured ISCO in a negative light, the stock would surely gap lower and I could lose anywhere from $50,000 to $100,000. It was an educated guess that the story would have a positive spin. The stock price rose into the market close, and I thought about taking risk-free profits of $5,000. Luckily, my greed overpowered my conservatism. My ego wouldn't let me sell for anything less than $20 per share, or $30,000 in profits.

I spent the weekend doing as much research as possible, happily discovering that the message boards were abuzz with anticipation. Everyone seemed to be thinking this company was the next Microsoft, and I knew such thinking would surely draw many buyers for me to sell into on Monday morning. Judging by this play's buzz, I wasn't the only one who'd made a large bet that the stock price would increase in the coming week.

I counted down the hours, minutes and seconds until it was time for the news program to air. When it finally aired, the show hyped ISCO's product perfectly, claiming they would single-handedly revolutionize the cell phone industry. I couldn't contain my enthusiasm. I stormed out of my dorm and ran around the quad screaming like a madman. When it came to trading, everyone already knew I was crazy, so they probably figured I had finally lost a bunch of money. In anticipation of the market open on Monday morning, I didn't sleep a wink Sunday night.

On Monday morning, when the prices began updating to account for the pre-market orders beginning at 8 a.m., I must have clicked my browser's refresh button at least a thousand times. Sure enough, ISCO was moving gradually higher by an average of an eighth of a point every few minutes. By 8:30 a.m., the pre-market stock price was $22 per share and I desperately wanted to sell, but I couldn't. Neither of my online discount brokerages allowed pre-market trading on OTCBB-listed companies. There was no doubt that this would be my biggest score ever. The only question was how fast could I sell my shares and convert my paper gains into real profits? Up until this time, my largest gain on any one trade had been $30,000. At ISCO's $22-per-share pre-market quote, this would be a $50,000 gain, my greatest victory yet. I wanted out quickly, so I called Suretrade to see if I could somehow be allowed to sell my shares before the market open.

While I was put on hold by Suretrade, ISCO's stock price just kept climbing. By 9 a.m., it had hit $24 per share, a potential gain of $70,000 for me. I finally got a Suretrade representative on the phone and hurriedly explained my situation. He was only a junior employee, so he had to check with his superiors to see if there was anything that could be done. Every second that ticked by seemed like an eternity. I sped up the pace of refreshing my quote screen.

By 9:15 a.m., the stock price had risen to $26 per share, and all I wanted to do was get out. I saw a few trades somehow sneak through as the trading volume showed a few hundred shares traded. Oh, how I wished those shares had been mine! As I expected, my Suretrade representative returned to tell me that I'd have to wait until the market open to sell. Before he even finished his explanation, I angrily hung up the phone and called my other broker, E*Trade. Their representative told me right away that I had no chance at selling during pre-market hours, so I gave up and turned my attention to the still climbing pre-market stock price. I was getting ready to submit sell orders for all my different accounts, but I needed to be sure to enter them after 9:30 a.m. because if they were placed even one second before that time, they'd be rejected as pre-market orders. I called several people and checked a few websites to verify that my clocks were accurate. I couldn't risk a potential trade rejection, since I'd then be forced to reload all my separate orders, and that would waste at least 30 seconds of perfectly good market action in which to sell my shares.

I timed it perfectly and successfully placed five sell orders within 10 seconds of the market open. The stock price was still climbing at 9:30 a.m. as ISCO was now trading at $27 per share—a $100,000 profit for me. I sat very still in my bathrobe, completely paralyzed, as if any movement might influence how quickly my orders would get filled. I repeatedly refreshed the open order buttons on my two trade platforms, but none of my orders seemed to be executing. The trading volume on ISCO had already surpassed 500,000 shares, but my tiny orders were being ignored.

By 9:37 a.m., the trading volume had surpassed the 1-million-share mark and I still hadn't sold any shares! By 9:40 a.m., I was back on the phone with Suretrade to see why my orders hadn't been executed. Just as a representative picked up, my Suretrade orders got executed. Without explaining, I immediately hung up and began calculating my gains. Suddenly, my E*Trade orders got executed, too.

All told, I sold my 10,000 shares at an average of $29.37 per share, a gain of $123,100. After commissions, my gain was $123,000 on the nose. The slowness of my order executions had actually helped me earn an extra $10,000. If I'd had the patience to wait another 15 minutes, I would've earned another $40,000.

After double-checking my accounts to make sure that I had indeed sold all my shares, I remained paralyzed in my chair for nearly 20 minutes. I repeatedly replayed the events of the previous few minutes in my head. My daily gain was more money than many well-educated people made in a year, and I was only a college freshman. I'd taken a great risk, and it'd paid off handsomely. I knew I wanted to celebrate that great moment, but the gain had occurred on the one day I had a morning class. The celebration would have to wait.

ISCO continued to climb that Monday and into Tuesday before peaking at $49.45. Their stock price then fell back to $15 that Wednesday and never saw double digits again because the company's revolutionary technology didn't take off. ISCO, now ISO, currently trades at 17¢ per share on the AMEX. Never underestimate the value of hype during a mania.

After this incredible triumph, I went straight to class, but I didn't hear a single word the professor said. I counted down the seconds until class was over so I could return to my dorm and tell everyone about my latest triumph.

I ran as fast as I could to beat my roommate back to the dorm, but he was already there, sitting innocently at his computer. He must've seen the crazy look in my eyes when he nervously asked how much I had made that day. I couldn't pretend that I hadn't made much this time around, so I blurted out, "$123,000!" His eyes became larger than I'd ever thought possible and I told him the whole story.

I decided that I wanted to do something extreme to celebrate this moment. An idea came to me right away. I told him to go round up the entire dorm because I wanted to take everyone out to a lavish dinner in downtown Boston. We eventually scrounged together three dozen or so freshmen who hopped onto a bus to make the journey. We dined at a fancy restaurant and had a grand ole time. The bill wasn't very high, coming in under $800. After all, other than one flask that somebody had snuck in, there was no alcohol involved, since we were all under 21!

This major trade lifted me to an entirely new plateau of confidence. I was now worth a little under $500,000 and had gained just over $350,000 in less than two months. In early 2000, I was earning approximately $175,000 per month, or almost $6,000 per day or about $250 per hour. If I kept up this pace, I would earn $2.1 million that year. This was all excluding taxes, which I didn't even want to think about. After all, these tremendous short-term trading profits elevated me to the much-dreaded 35% tax bracket, and my being a Connecticut resident added another 4%. Just a few weeks earlier, I'd already taken some money out of my accounts to pay taxes, but my parents now made me withdraw $70,000 more for tax purposes. I was shocked by the speed with which I had made so much money, but it didn't stop me from continuing to trade aggressively. It was during the next few weeks that I would enjoy the single best run of my entire trading career.

Trading during the last week of February and the first two weeks of March 2000 can only be described as surreal. The market's mania went into overdrive and finally reached what would be its pinnacle. This three-week period seemed to fly by as the trades came faster than ever on the greatest trading volume I'd ever seen. One week before, the daily trading volumes on my target stocks had reached only 10 million shares, but now were reaching the 30-, 40- and sometimes even the 50-million-share marks. I could hardly believe my eyes, but I took advantage of this circus nonetheless. The combination of my newfound wealth, supreme confidence, phenomenal liquidity and the unbelievable volatility in the OTCBB marketplace allowed me to take even larger positions of 20,000 to 30,000 shares, which, as always, I divided among my five accounts.

During this period, I traded more than 70 different plays, almost all of them following the same gap-up strategy. Stock prices now gapped higher by 50¢, 75¢ and sometimes even $1 per share. Multiply those price gains by my average position of 25,000 shares, and you'll be able to understand how I made over $350,000 during those three weeks alone. Yes, that averages out to $116,667 per week, $23,333 per trading day, $3,589 per trading hour or $60 per trading minute! To add to the absurdity of these gains, I didn't even have many losses during this stretch.

My greatest trading losses never exceeded a few thousand dollars, while my largest gains cleared $50,000 apiece. The best part of this streak was that the plays didn't warrant much research because these were mostly the same stocks I'd been playing for the previous few months. This was their final run-up during the mania, and each one seemingly wanted to go out with a bang. I was completely in sync with this market environment, and my trading had never been better.

The hype-fueled marketplace peaked in mid-March 2000, and although it made a valiant effort to reach new highs later in the month, the breakout failed and the market's gradual descent began. I cannot pinpoint the exact date on which I stopped making $23,333 per trading day, but as the market declined further, there were far fewer gap-up plays because nobody wanted to risk any potential gap-downs.

After all, these trading opportunities relied on the strength of the overall market for their existence. I'd always bought before the market close and sold near the market open the next day, but now the pattern mutated. Now I couldn't buy at the same time because other traders had already bought in anticipation of the end-of-the-day run-up. Stocks began surging with 10 minutes of trading before the market close, and then a few days later, they would surge with 30 minutes to go. A few days more and I needed to buy as early as one hour before the market close to avoid the inevitable run-up. The pattern's mutation was forcing me to buy earlier to beat the crowd, but the crowd wasn't dumb, so it gradually began buying earlier, too.

By the end of March 2000, we were all buying so early before the market close and selling so quickly at the market open the next day that the best time to take solid gains now was before the market close. The marketplace matured to make holding positions overnight an unprofitable strategy. Stock prices began gapping lower in the mornings because the tremendous number of incoming sell orders outweighed the incoming buy orders. This market inefficiency collapsed under the weight of too many traders playing the same game.

I'm sure the strategy's collapse was due in part to the popularity of my message board, which had now grown to over 9,000 members. I'd already closed my newsletter because too many people were asking me for advice. I stopped checking other boards because nearly every single post was fluff, hype or spam. Since starting to make the big bucks, I'd stopped posting on my own board, but I couldn't help checking in from time to time. The fluff had now overwhelmed my board, too. There was so much money to be made in this little niche that amateurs of all kinds had become the most active members. Other traders took charge of the board, and, unlike me, they didn't seem to mind the madness surrounding them.

One day, I'd had enough, and in frustration, I deleted the entire group. I would've allowed it to implode on its own, but I didn't want the newer traders to be able to look at the older posts and copy my successful trading strategies. I doubted anybody from the new bunch would even have the brains to do that, but why chance it? Thousands of traders now played this little niche, and their presence overloaded my beloved, consistently profitable gap-up strategy. If I hadn't created the group, would this pattern have lasted another week? Maybe it would've lasted another two weeks? Or maybe even another month? Who knows, but I'd clearly let too many people know about all this easy money. The pattern was so profitable near its end that one extra week would be the equivalent of over $100,000 in profits. The creation of my board inadvertently hurt my chances to make further gains. I learned that if I wanted to make money trading, I should never tell anybody about my trading strategies again.

A trader's ability to adapt to changing market conditions is the key to successful trading. Once I saw my profits fall, I adjusted to the new environment and took smaller positions. I even managed to make a few thousand dollars in the final few days before my strategy imploded. Of course, I lost those profits and more rather quickly when I pushed my luck a little too much at the very end, but overall, I managed to hold onto the vast majority of my gains. By the beginning of April 2000, I had made over $720,000 for the year and there was $840,000 sitting in cash— before taxes—in my five accounts.

As impressive as these figures were, I knew I'd have to hand over a great deal of my newfound wealth to the IRS. My accountant made sure to tell my parents to make me pay my quarterly taxes on time, and I ended up writing a rather large check to the IRS. I was practically in tears as I scribbled out the check that exceeded $300,000, or 40% of all my gains from the previous 15 months. Yes, it had been barely more than a year since I was worth a little over $10,000 and now I had 50 times that amount, even after taxes. Life was sweet, and it was about to get even sweeter as I watched the vast majority of the other nouveau riche lose the greater part of their wealth over the next few months.

While many praised my foresight, they mistook my incredible luck for incredible intelligence. I didn't know the crash was coming. The price action in my target stocks simply didn't offer any trading opportunities, so I was forced to sit on the sidelines. Still, I congratulated myself and began imagining what my life would be like if I could pull in $700,000 annually. I couldn't stop talking about the beauty of my short holding periods, thinking I'd be able to trade profitably in any market environment whatsoever.

Of course, I was in for a rude awakening as the market's fall sapped the potential for any great trading opportunities for the foreseeable future. The volatility and liquidity in the microcap marketplace disappeared almost entirely.

I knew my gap-up strategy was over for the time being, so I began looking for new strategies from which to profit. I looked at commodities, currencies and options, but they all seemed very foreign to me. After a few weeks of research, I concluded I wouldn't be able to compete effectively in those marketplaces. After all, they were home to some of the richest and best-informed speculators on the planet, who frequently indulged in great leverage. Considering the competition, I didn't see any way I could make the kind of consistent trading profits to which I'd become accustomed. I preferred playing in a smaller, more inefficient arena, so I returned to searching through my favorite OTCBB-listed companies for new patterns and opportunities.

Regrettably, there were no longer any plays that seemed the least bit interesting in the niche I loved so dearly. The trading volume had dried up with amazing speed, so I wouldn't even be able to trade with any size if anything interesting did eventually materialize. The volatility in this marketplace now seemed to pertain exclusively to the downside, especially since many articles were now published that detailed so-called pump-and-dump schemes.

I'd heard about pump-and-dumps before, but I'd never really looked into them in detail. Now that I had a good deal of time on my hands, I decided to do some digging. What I discovered shocked me to my core.

Apparently, the majority of the OTCBB-listed companies I played had been involved in several variations of manipulative schemes. I knew the business fundamentals on many of my target stocks had been less than stellar, especially since the Federal Bureau of Investigation had raided the offices of several of my plays, but I had no idea as to the extent of the price manipulation that went on behind the scenes. Financial publications and SEC filings enlightened me as to the incredible dealings of these manipulators, and I devoured each article in astonishment.

Stock promoters, marketing firms and sometimes company executives themselves received, owned or bought hundreds of thousands and sometimes millions of shares of these tiny companies and then, using all sorts of methods, proceeded to pump their stock prices higher. These newly published articles detailed how pumpers used message board posts, press releases, e-mail and fax spam and boiler rooms to promote the stocks in which they had positions. They'd send out tens of thousands and sometimes even hundreds of thousands of e-mails, faxes and direct mailings to unsuspecting people, billing the stocks in which they had positions as incredible investment opportunities. The SEC had gone after several promoters who exaggerated or lied in their claims; one of them was just a teenager like me. He'd posted thousands of messages on various message boards by using dozens of fake aliases, convincing others to buy his stocks through spirited debates among his many different profiles. As impressive as his scheme was, I couldn't help feel somewhat proud of myself for never having crossed that line. For once, my inherent scrappiness was subdued by pride. Such tactics helped pull off the manipulation schemes of these stock promoters, but *boiler rooms* enjoyed the greatest success.

Boiler rooms were shady brokerage houses that existed solely to pump the owners' stocks. The "brokers" at these boiler rooms often earned incredible commissions, cold-calling people from all walks of life in the hopes of convincing them to buy the stocks they were promoting. They frequently called people who had little industry knowledge but big dreams of making money in the stock market. It wasn't very difficult to convince people to buy shares in their stocks because the boiler rooms knew that people wanted to participate in the market's rise even if it meant risking their financial security. So, the boiler rooms would offer people "sure things," claiming that their picks involved little to no risk.

Brokers frequently called their targets around dinnertime to have the greatest chances of finding somebody at home to take their phone call. If the brokers were successful in their pitches and the targets wanted to buy the stock immediately, a buy order would be placed before the market open the next day. Hence, the pileup of pre-market orders and nearly the entire reason for the gap-up plays that had made so much money for me. While I'm sure that many people were still skeptical after they first received a boiler room phone call, some eventually consented because they must've seen the stocks mentioned consistently increasing in price. The boiler rooms would keep calling back every few days to say "I told you so" until the target was persuaded to want to buy the stock. It was like taking candy from a baby as the boiler rooms preyed upon the greed of so many unfortunate investors.

The boiler rooms' target stocks were manipulated higher because the success of their operation depended on sucking in new customers daily. It was usually only a few weeks after customers had bought the stock that the rug was pulled out from under them. Once the boiler rooms stopped promoting their target stock, the demand and subsequently the stock price collapsed. After all, boiler rooms needed to manipulate a stock only until they could liquidate their position before moving on to their next play and prey. It was a vicious cycle as the stocks they promoted surged from a few cents to many dollars per share before eventually falling back down again. The boiler rooms' customers were left holding the bag, losing most of what they invested nearly every time. Apparently, my perfectly uptrending stocks were perfect for a reason; they were being manipulated to appear that way.

After reading through all the sordid details, I was in shock. I'd known about stock manipulation, but I hadn't imagined its being indirectly responsible for my incredible gains. I could live with promoters, hype-filled press releases and message board fluff because they were all easy to spot, but boiler rooms represented an entirely different level of manipulation. Their presence was nearly impossible to track. There simply wasn't any way to tell who was doing all the buying unless I'd known somebody working for the boiler rooms themselves. This brought me back to the many sleepless nights I'd spent wondering who was behind all the mysterious buying power of my target stocks. I now had my answer and it wasn't pretty.

Since many of the boiler rooms were linked to organized crime, did my newfound wealth place me on an organized crime watch list? Was I now on the SEC's watch list? I hadn't been in cahoots with the nefarious side of the marketplace, but could I prove my innocence in a court of law? Would anybody believe I could make all that money based on my pattern recognition abilities alone? I suddenly grew concerned.

After a few days, my fears subsided and reason kicked in. I was simply a speculator who took advantage of price patterns. Boiler rooms were just one example of the many catalysts that created patterns in the stock market. Inevitably, other catalysts would emerge and I could profit from their influence, too. As long as there was enough volatility and liquidity in the marketplace, I'd be golden. Unfortunately, once the bubble burst, those two variables disappeared altogether and there didn't appear to be any other opportunities for easy gains for the time being. I was almost sad to see these criminals get busted. I felt bad for the boiler rooms' many victims, but the victims' losses were their own fault: a direct result of greed, ignorance and laziness.

Now I knew it was time for me to leave this marketplace and seek opportunities elsewhere. I sadly closed down three of my five online discount brokerage accounts and said good-bye to the niche that had given me so much.

Chapter 7: When the Levees Broke

By mid-April 2000, the NASDAQ had plummeted 25%, but the most popular technology stocks remained as volatile as ever. Even as prices dropped, people still didn't give up on these stocks, and their resultant dip buying created frequent price spikes. I decided to devote myself to learning how to profit from this volatility because I didn't know how long it would last. I figured I'd have to endure minor trading losses in the beginning, but I was cocky enough to believe that I could tackle any new market segment, given enough time. Even though this marketplace and its companies were exponentially more complex than those traded on the OTCBB, I thought my pattern recognition abilities would

eventually lead me to discover new opportunities. I also wanted
to satisfy my ego by reaching the $1-million earnings mark by
year's end. To reach this goal, I needed to make only an additional $280,000 during the next eight months: that shouldn't be
so difficult, right? I was in for a big surprise.

I started trading the most popular technology-related
stocks, and almost immediately, I began losing money. For educational purposes, I'd anticipated taking some short-term losses,
but my losses quickly exceeded all previous expectations. Now,
nearly 75% of my recent trades were resulting in losses. I did one
thing right by forcing myself to take small positions, so even if
my losses were great in number, they were small in size. After
all, I couldn't allow these test trades to dent my precious net
worth; my ego wouldn't allow it. I traded shares of Sun, Cisco,
Yahoo!, Intel and Juniper—basically, any well-known technology company whose stock price displayed great volatility. I tried
applying my OTCBB trading rules to this marketplace but
without the same success. No matter what type of price patterns
I played—whether they were *breakouts* (stocks hitting new highs),
breakdowns (stocks hitting new lows), *dips* (stocks dropping
quickly), *short squeezes* (stocks spiking higher due to panicking
short sellers), *fades* (stocks falling after gap-ups), *bounces* (stocks
rebounding from dips), *spikes* (stocks surging quickly), *gap-ups*
or *gap-downs*—nothing seemed to work with any consistency. I
even tried taking a value approach by buying seemingly undervalued companies, but this also produced only mixed results. I
read analyst reports by the hundreds, but their opinions varied
greatly. I thought of these reports as basically a more advanced
form of message board hype, except that these analysts were paid

for their "research." In the end, there didn't seem to be any kind of consensus whatsoever.

These test trades cost me only a few thousand dollars in losses, but it felt like much more, considering it'd been only a few weeks since I had been enjoying weekly gains of $100,000. I had to face the fact that the game had changed. Was this due to the market's recent downfall? Maybe these price patterns just didn't work with larger companies. Maybe the mania had truly ended and business fundamentals would matter from here on out. Whatever the case, it didn't matter because I was done with trading for now. It was demoralizing. But I couldn't make any money in this new environment unless I took on a great amount of risk. Since I had lost money on nearly all of the recent trading strategies I'd tested, I decided I wouldn't stupidly risk any large amounts of money for now. The risk-reward ratio just wasn't in my favor.

I had made a great deal of money very quickly, but did that mean I was now destined to be a full-time financial professional? Had I been lucky, or did I really have a talent for trading? The vast majority of amateur traders lost money, but I had always done extremely well; what made me so special? Would it be possible to find new profit opportunities, or was I destined to be a one-hit wonder? I was tired of trying to find answers to these questions. Right now I just wanted to relax. I decided to take some time off and finally enjoy some of my newfound wealth.

In mid-April 2000, I traveled to New Orleans to visit one of my best friends from high school at Tulane University. New Orleans turned out to be the perfect destination to forget all my worries as I drowned myself in alcohol, partying and girls. The girls were actually good-looking down there, and the weather was beautiful—not a bad combination at all. It was paradise compared to Tufts. I'd planned on staying for a few days but I was having so much fun that I extended my vacation. I knew I'd miss some classes, but I figured I would've missed them anyway if I kept up with my trading. Of course, instead of watching the markets stuck in my dorm room because of the freezing cold weather back at Tufts, I was now using a laptop to watch the markets at the Tulane pool surrounded by beautiful girls in beautiful weather. Yes, I preferred watching the markets poolside. In fact, the near-tropical surroundings made me question why I'd attended Tufts in the first place.

I liked Tulane so much, I immediately looked into transferring. Unlike most colleges, Tulane still accepted fall transfers even though it was already late in the season. Tufts was a better college than Tulane, at least academically, but did that even really matter anymore? How much did I value my academic future now that I had found a profession with the potential to make me rich? I knew my $500,000 in cash wouldn't last me the rest of my life and that I'd eventually have to find a job, but I also realized that I was now set for the foreseeable future. I just needed to make sure I didn't blow this security blanket with any excessive spending or reckless trading.

Tufts might help me get a better job in the long run, but was that really worth three more years of suffering? I was majoring in economics, and as much as that helped in trading, I hated it. There was no doubt in my mind. I wanted to enroll in a business school, and Tulane had one; Tufts did not. After all, I'd only

gone to Tufts for its reputation, but with my latest accomplish-
ments, who cared about a school's reputation? Now I had my
own. My only concern was my trading, so I needed to choose a
college that would best complement this new passion of mine.
Tulane was a perfect fit, with its stress-free environment, perfect
weather, good-looking girls, easy academic course load and business school. I applied and was accepted for the fall semester.

During the summer of 2000, my trading was worse than
ever. I wasn't losing much money, but I wasn't making any either. No matter how many business books I read or how much
research I did, my returns were lackluster. I'd gone through cold
streaks before, but I still never got used to it. While at home
in Connecticut, I tried to take some time off from trading and
relax, but I couldn't. I desperately wanted to break the $1-million
earnings mark before year's end, and until I accomplished that
goal, I struggled to think of anything else.

After settling into Tulane in the fall, I still traded daily,
but without much success. Neither my new location nor lower
stress levels seemed to matter. I tested every trading strategy
imaginable, but I found nothing worked with any consistency. I
resorted to beefing up my market knowledge by dedicating myself to reading every article on every trading and financial website
I could find. I was shocked that there was absolutely nothing on
penny stocks or microcap companies. I learned a great deal about
other industries, but despite all my newfound trading wisdom,
profits were still few and far between. I turned to reading business biographies; surely, other traders had endured this kind of
cold streak at some point during their careers. I was right. Even

the most successful speculators had experienced difficult times; all I needed was a little patience. Unfortunately, that was something I sorely lacked.

After a few weeks of further research, I thought I'd discovered a great strategy: buying fundamentally sound companies after their stock prices had plunged. I enjoyed many small gains when I first began using this strategy, but, sadly, a $49,000 loss on one of these types of plays cancelled out all my initial gains. This was the largest loss I had ever taken. Apparently, some seemingly undervalued stocks could fall further in price, no matter if their business fundamentals supported higher prices.

Lesson learned, back to the drawing board. My trading lacked focus as I began trading whatever was hot regardless of whether the company was large or small. I craved the warm feeling that consistent profits brought me. I needed to control myself. But it was no use; I was weak. Luckily, it was then that I discovered *short selling*.

After reading about this trading strategy in several books, I tried short selling for the first time. To take positions in stocks, instead of buying shares like most investors did, short sellers borrowed from their broker shares they didn't own in order to sell short these borrowed shares. It was basically like taking negative positions in stocks to capture profits from any downside price action. To exit their short positions, short sellers aimed to buy their shares back at lower stock prices. If stock prices rose, short sellers lost money because they'd be forced to buy their shares back at the higher prices after they'd already sold their shares at lower prices. Short selling boiled down to simply buying and sell-

ing stocks like everybody else, but the order was reversed because
short sellers sold first and bought back later. Short selling was
considered riskier than buying, or *going long*, because, theoretically, stock prices could surge infinitely higher, while they could
only drop to zero on the downside. Thus, short sellers could lose
everything in addition to actually owing money to their broker if
their trades went sour.

At first, I couldn't wrap my mind around these concepts;
the idea of taking negative positions in stocks sounded crazy.
But after a few days, it made a great deal of sense to me because
I knew that many stocks deserved to trade at much lower prices
and sometimes even worthy stocks fell dramatically. It was nice
to now be able to profit if and when stock prices fell.

While I began liking the basic idea of this strategy, its ap-
plication was tricky and would take time to master. Still, I desperately needed to try something new because after eight months
of experimenting with dozens of different trading strategies, I
had lost a total of $10,000. Only during the final few days of the
year did I finally resign myself to the fact that I wouldn't top the
$1-million earnings mark in 2000. The good news was that even
as the overall market tanked through the latter part of the year,
I hadn't lost much money. Others had lost fortunes. Defying all
bullish expectations, the NASDAQ lost nearly one-third of its
value within a few months.

The new year brought a quick bounce in the overall markets
as the decline over the previous few months had been gruel-
ing but gradual. It was during this time that I became a bona
fide short seller by focusing on betting against the most popular
technology-related stocks. During the fall, they had been hit the

hardest, so now they bounced the quickest. I believed this bounce lacked conviction and occurred too quickly. Some people couldn't wait to buy these stocks at discount prices, so they bought too early. Over the previous few months, many more people had lost so much money that they were looking to sell their shares on any bounce in order to take what money they could out of the stock market. I believed that if the bounce started to crack even a little, panic selling would likely ensue, thus creating many great short selling opportunities. It was a beautiful time to be a short seller, as there was a sense of desperation in the air. The environment seemed ripe for the picking.

At first, I began short selling these stocks by using only a little money, taking 1,000-share positions at a time. After all, I was a true amateur short seller, but I'd short stocks that had bounced considerably and seemed ready for reversals. From the start, I was very successful with this strategy as the widespread fear in the overall market cut through stock prices like a warm knife through butter. The rallies in technology stocks collapsed with alarming speed, and I closed my short positions, or *covered*, for solid profits. I dared not hold too long, for my main goal was just to prove that I could trade profitably once again. As usual, I covered my short positions too early, but as my profits grew in size, I gradually became more comfortable with this new strategy and held larger positions for longer periods of time.

Short selling opportunities were easy to spot. I simply looked for stocks that fell the hardest, bounced the quickest and now appeared ready to reverse lower again. Most of my new target plays were technology companies, but as always, I didn't

discriminate as to which industries I played. Around this time,
I discovered stock-screening software that enabled me to screen
thousands of different price patterns in bulk. Meticulously scan-
ning through all these patterns sounds very boring, but I thoroughly enjoyed scouring the landscape for my prey.

The OTCBB market still lacked volatility and liquidity, so
instead, I focused on NASDAQ- and AMEX-listed companies.
Luckily, the overall market cooperated, selling off sharply into
every single bounce, and my new target stocks sold off, in turn,
with the overall market.

With little resistance, the most popular technology stocks
continued their descent. I began noticing that the price drops
grew particularly steep around 10 a.m. and 2 p.m. I began short
selling specifically at those times of day, and the results were
amazing. I had no idea why those times were important, but as
usual, I simply traded in tune with the patterns I discovered. I
particularly enjoyed short selling stocks that opened higher after
three or four days of solid gains but whose trading volumes had
begun to fade. Without as many buyers, these stocks frequently
dropped in price soon after the market open. When a stock's
price change remained slightly negative on the day for a few minutes and failed to bounce, I'd short even more shares because this
meant that people were hesitant to buy, fearing a potentially large
price drop. In this case, within a few minutes after the market
open, stock prices would crash lower as panicking investors sold
their shares simultaneously. This, I learned, was a popular trading
pattern called a *gap and trap*. Momentum traders got "trapped"
in their positions when their stocks were unable to hold any gains
after the market open.

Another favorite short selling pattern that worked well for me was what I like to call the *afternoon fade*. In the morning, many of my target stocks would be more volatile because nobody knew how they would perform for the day. In the morning, traders would still be adjusting their expectations to reflect company or industry news from the pre-market or the night before. But by the afternoon, the day's news would be fully digested, limiting a stock's movement to a tight price range. The afternoon fade occurred after a strong stock would turn slightly negative on the day. If the stock price had moved sharply higher over the previous few days, there would be a great deal of room for the stock price to fall after the momentum faded.

To protect them from the risk of further downside, many investors would use *stop losses*, or orders that automatically sold investors out of their positions when a stock price breached a predetermined level. As a stock would breach one of these important levels, thousands of computer-automated stop-loss orders would light up, looking to sell as quickly as possible. This onslaught of simultaneous selling would depress a stock price for however long it took for the entire batch of sell orders to be executed. Within seconds or minutes, stock prices would drop sharply, sometimes by as much as $2 to $3 per share, because the few buyers present didn't want to buy directly into the tsunami of sellers. These massive selling onslaughts would scare buyers because the resulting price action was surprisingly similar to companies that announced negative news. When that happened, stocks would sell-off sharply. While it was impossible to know exactly where these stop-loss orders amassed, due to the popularity of do-it-yourself investment books, many investors had been taught to place them at nice round numbers like $20 or $40 per share, so these important price levels were rather predictable.

I took great pleasure in short selling into these key price levels, riding the wave of sellers as their computer-automated orders pushed stock prices lower. I covered my short positions and took my profits wherever buyers finally emerged. I never had the patience to ride the whole selling wave, but I still profited quite a bit.

Before short selling, I waited for these price patterns to occur because it's extremely difficult to short into strong stocks. After all, there's a reason why more than 90% of short sellers lose money; momentum stocks often rise much further than expected. The key to successful short selling is to wait for signs that indicate the momentum may be over, at least for the time being.

For me, the most reliable indicator to prepare for the possibility of short selling is when strong stocks exhibit prolonged *sideways price action*. Sideways price action occurs when a stock trades in a tight price range without breaking out. It tells me that sellers have entered the marketplace and buyers may become fearful that a reversal is near. They may switch their allegiance to become sellers themselves, providing more ammunition that helps prevent further price strength. If the sideways price action turns into downward price action, strong stocks drop quickly because the reversal is now confirmed. Sometimes these types of price breakdowns occur, but the stock price still tries to bounce back higher. Now these stocks will either resume their upward trending—forcing short sellers to cover their positions, or buy back their borrowed shares—or run into a wall of sellers, preventing any further price increase. If the latter occurs, short sellers usually gain confidence and add to their positions because this pattern is known as a *double top*. A double top is a highly reliable price pattern, and if it occurs, it's a probable sign that further price weakness lies ahead.

The overall market was still in a free fall and my target stocks took the brunt of the selling, so I probably was too conservative to require these intraday patterns to develop before short selling. Then again, I was still new to short selling, so I needed to follow my rules to ensure success. It was amazing to watch these patterns develop, as I could almost picture the frantic mutual fund managers, investors and day traders hysterically dumping their positions in unison. In this market environment, the intraday values of many large technology companies could swing by 20 to 30%. Within a few months' time, the stocks of many of the largest technology companies lost over 70% of their market values.

If I'd been more experienced in short selling, my gains would've been much larger, but instead, I was comfortable taking small intraday gains. I aimed to make 5 to 10% on each trade, but I usually ended up taking profits after I had made only 2 or 3%. Even though I believed my target stocks would probably continue to slump, I craved consistent profits, so these small gains fit the bill. When I looked at my computer monitors to see the little green numbers indicating how much money I had made, I felt a momentary burst of exhilaration. I knew few people, if any, were making money in this market environment, so my profits made me feel rather special.

By now, albeit a bit wiser and more conservative, I found myself once again with the perfect strategy at the perfect time in stock market history. While I continually left thousands of dollars in potential profits on the table, I earned a respectable $75,000 during the first three months of 2001. I wasn't aiming for home runs, because I now believed the big money days were behind me. While I continued to trade profitably, I wouldn't risk large amounts of capital for fear of damaging my now $550,000 after-tax net worth. With this new strategy, I had already successfully played dozens of stocks, but my average gain per trade was only $2,000. To reduce the risk of any potential news or overall market bounce, I rarely held overnight, but I was especially scared because I never knew if or when the bear market would end. After all, unlike the OTCBB-listed companies, these were real companies, so there had to be a bottom somewhere. Or so I assumed.

While I was usually patient enough to wait for the proper price action to occur before short selling, sometimes the price drops stopped cold in their tracks and reversed back higher too quickly for me to avoid losses. This was not some tiny market niche; many people played this game, and their trading created many fakeouts.

When these price spikes occurred, short sellers tried to buy to cover their positions and avoid nasty losses, but their buying only helped push stock prices higher. This pattern is known as a *short squeeze*. Momentum traders crave this pattern because they know panicking short sellers can create quick price surges. They jump aboard too, and their buying pushes stock prices even higher, "squeezing" the shorts even more. These situations, while rare, scare most traders away from short selling, since the losses can add up quickly.

Throughout the summer of 2001, I continued to be successful in short selling my target stocks. This strategy, while not as consistently profitable as my gap-up strategy, helped me earn another $125,000 during the summer. This pushed my yearly income to $200,000 heading into the fall. I was relieved to be making some decent money once again.

Then 9/11 hit.

Due to the fact that I'd stayed up late the night before, researching potential plays, I was sound asleep when my room-mate burst into my room to tell me what had happened. I joined several mesmerized friends in watching the news for nearly two straight days. And I learned the stock market would be closed for several days.

As shocked as I was, I used the time off to scan through the message boards to see which stocks would be most affected. While I felt the shock and sadness experienced by all Americans, I immediately thought of this as a trading opportunity. There were dozens of companies that were being touted as the main beneficiaries, so I decided to keep track of them all. I knew the markets would be volatile, but I underestimated just how pan-icked everybody would be.

When the markets reopened, the stock prices of several security companies rose exponentially, while the overall market dropped nearly 15%. As much as I wanted to join in the action one way or the other, I was paralyzed. I'd never seen such pan-demonium, so I played it safe by watching the action from the sidelines. It was difficult to sit back and do nothing, but this was some scary stuff.

It was the right move.

The market rebounded sharply and my target stocks ex-tended their run-ups. If I had shorted into the brief period of price weakness and timed my trades perfectly, I might've made some money, but I would've lost a great deal more during the snapback rally. My chances of success were slim because even under ideal conditions, my timing was almost always off. If I had shorted into the continuing price strength, I would've been squeezed alongside many other short sellers and lost even more money. So, I watched in astonishment, realizing some short squeezes do not end quickly.

Up until that time, I'd only read about the great short squeezes of the past. I had always traded conservatively enough to avoid the possibility of being squeezed. In the fall of 2001, this changed as my confidence in my short selling abilities had grown in tandem with the size of the positions I took.

In October, I was trading somewhat aggressively while the market continued its free fall. The most popular technology-related stocks were still in the gutter—that is, except for a few stubborn plays. The stock prices of these lucky few surged higher as short sellers piled on in disbelief. So far, I had stayed on the sidelines during these types of run-ups, but I thought I perceived a crack in the intraday price strength of one of these plays, so I excitedly jumped in and took a small short position.

Earlier in the year, from its previous high of $105, this stock had fallen to the $30 range, but it had now risen to the $90 range. The stock was very actively traded, so I tried *scalping* it for a few dollars per share with a small position. Scalping is the art of trying to profit from sudden intraday price moves, with the goal being to make a few cents per share. At first, I shorted only 300 shares but *averaged my position higher*—or sold more shares short at higher prices to average my cost basis up— as the stock price surged higher against me. I knew a break in price was inevitable, but the question was how much pain would I be able to stand before the stock finally cracked?

I was in the red only a few dollars per share, so I kept averaging my cost basis higher to give myself a chance to profit or at least to break even. My stubbornness and ego combined to allow me to grow my short position to 5,000 shares. I should've taken this small loss because it would've been insignificant in the large scheme of things, but instead, I now risked nearly 75% of my net worth on the hunch that I was right. To this day, I can't figure out why. Still, I was confident that the stock price would fall sooner or later, so I held my position firm. I ignored all my risk management rules regarding holding overnight and taking quick losses to prevent larger losses. My loss was still minimal and yet I had held for nearly three trading days, which was an eternity for me. I just couldn't give in; this was now a personal battle between the stock and me. I wouldn't let any pesky rules stand in the way of my glory.

But, as the stock price surged higher, my resolve weakened and I was forced to absorb a $36,000 loss. I had lost nearly $6 per share and I just couldn't stand the pain any longer. My exit point in the $96 price range turned out to be a rather good exit, but this one positive action clearly didn't make up for my ridiculous stubbornness that caused the loss in the first place. The stock had shown a glimmer of weakness but quickly turned against me. I ignored the price strength while trying to rationalize my position and looking for anything that would support my ego-based rationale. My ego got the best of me and led me to believe I had psychic abilities as to how the stock would act even as the price action suggested otherwise.

I had made a great deal of money predicting future stock prices, but I'd always had the price action on my side. There's a big difference between price-action-based trading and ego-based trading. Price-action-based trading doesn't ensure profits every time, but the odds are better because it's at least based on research and reason. Ego-based trading rarely succeeds, and when it does, it's the result of sheer luck because it's not supported by rationality.

Over the next few days, this stock continued to rise, but it hit a perfect double top at $105. A few months later, the company released negative news and their stock price dropped all the way to $45. For a split second, I felt guilty about not being short during this incredible price drop, but that just wasn't my game. Stocks will always make large moves without me; I just needed to be involved when the probability was on my side.

A few days later, as I was anxious for a chance at redemption, another short selling opportunity appeared. This was another high-flying technology company that never received the memo about its being a bear market. This stock had actually broken out to make a new all-time high but looked as though it would come back down, since the intraday trading volume had already begun to fade. Due to the strength of the pattern that indicated the stock price would soon head lower, I quickly loaded up by selling short 20,000 shares. It was a lowly priced stock, so I used only approximately 30% of my net worth on the position. Heading into the market close, I had a paper profit of $3,000, so I'd have to decide whether to take this small gain or hold my position overnight. I was still cocky enough to believe I could succeed even while breaking the very rules that were meant to protect me, so I held my position overnight.

The next day, the stock price dropped perfectly at the market open, but I still didn't cover my short position. I had a paper profit of only $22,000, which wouldn't make up for my other loss a few days before. I promised myself that I would hold until I broke even from these two trades. My paper profit now surged to $27,000, but I still didn't take it. What an idiot. Within 10 minutes, my $27,000 paper profit had now turned into a $6,000 paper loss. If I didn't cover my short, the stock price could rise further against me, creating an even larger loss. I couldn't chance another reversal in my favor, so I decided to cut my losses while they were still somewhat small. Unfortunately, many other shorts were trying to cover too, so I joined them in trying to cover their short positions.

I'd always used *limit orders*, or orders executed at or below specified prices, so I immediately placed my orders to close my position. I still traded with two accounts so it was easier for me to input my orders, but the stock price rose too quickly for my limit orders to be executed. I found myself placing several new limit orders, but I was just chasing the stock price higher. It simply wouldn't stop going up! I eventually panicked and placed my limit nearly 25¢ above the current stock price. There was a flurry of buying and I was finally out. I had panicked at the worst possible point, because it was only seconds later that the stock price quickly dropped back to my breakeven point. Unfortunately, I had already taken a $28,600 loss.

I'd made a common short selling mistake. While everyone else was panicking, that was the time to trade in the opposite direction. Instead, I panicked along with everybody else and suffered the consequences. Now I had lost $64,000, all because of my inability to abide by my self-imposed rules. There was no doubt in my mind: I needed to learn to become a more disci-

plined trader. There was another lesson here: whenever you have
a solid profit, take it. Don't try to set specific profit goals, because
that will get you into trouble. Not content to accept these failures,
I wanted to prove to myself that I hadn't lost my edge, so I immediately began looking for new plays.

Luckily, at the time, I was reading a trading book that advised readers to take a break after any large trading loss. The book
made many good points, and the author seemed to be speaking
directly to me. I wouldn't be aiming for a small profit now because
I could only think about getting my money back—and that was
the worst motivation for trading. I stopped looking for new plays
and concentrated on reading. Within a week, I'd finished that
book and two other books on trading psychology. They opened
my eyes to the factors that had hurt my trading performance for
so long and, more importantly, had helped me take a much-need-
ed break from trading. By the end of my weeklong trading hiatus,
my mind was once again open to taking small gains instead of
trying to earn back all my losses in one or two trades.

When a new short selling opportunity presented itself,
I was ready. This time I was determined to trade by the book,
literally. I calmly reviewed all possible price scenarios and overall
market conditions, and I researched the company thoroughly. After all this, I felt confident in taking a short position, and quickly
took a large one. Not completely by the books, I admit. The books
didn't support my decision to take such a large position so quickly,
but I remained confident nonetheless. I risked nearly half my
capital and yet I knew no matter what happened, I wouldn't hold
overnight. This was just a test trade, albeit a large one, to see if I
could follow my trading rules, or at least the majority of them.

Fortunately, I was completely right about this play. By the afternoon, the stock and the overall market had faded perfectly. I covered my short position before the market close with an 8% profit, or nearly $30,000. I actually covered near the bottom of the stock's price range, so I was extremely proud of this trade. The stock price acted exactly how I thought it would. Even though I was still down on the whole from my previous three trades, I felt as if I had crossed some sort of experience threshold as a trader and that my future results would reflect this newfound strength.

Over the next few weeks, I experienced my greatest string of profitable trades since the easy-money days, trading nearly two dozen plays with profits totaling $25,000. The profits weren't as great as before, but my 2001 yearly earnings of $170,000 were still pretty good for a kid in the middle of his junior year in college.

As much as I enjoyed my new trading strategy, I enjoyed my time at Tulane even more. I'd definitely chosen wisely. The bars stayed open late, so I eagerly participated in the local night-life. The wild parties, free-flowing alcohol and crazy party girls combined to take the edge off my daily operations. Even though I loved going out and meeting people at bars and clubs, I never really made many close friends. This was due in part to my decision to major in philosophy and take night classes in order to focus on trading during the daytime. Originally, I'd transferred to take advantage of Tulane's business school, but I'd become more interested in philosophy because I believed it to be a way to diversify my knowledge base. I still pursued a business minor, but since I didn't take very many business classes, I never really became friendly with any business majors. In my night classes, I was stuck with philosophy students who were mostly adults or just plain weird.

I tried to expand my social circle by pledging a fraternity, but trading ruined that too. During pledge week, a brother called to ask me to bring two dozen eggs to him immediately. Unfortunately, I couldn't go anywhere because I was in the middle of an important trade and I told him so. Apparently, that was the wrong answer and I didn't get in. I made $1,500 on the trade instead. My trading still came first and I was willing to sacrifice my social life for it.

I made it my New Year's resolution that 2002 would be a year of intense market study. I'd been trading too often—foolishly wasting my time with unworthy plays—because I needed to stroke my ego with consistent profits. I was now worth over $600,000, after taxes, so these trades offered little upside. I needed to control my profit cravings and focus on trades that had greater potential. Since I wanted to focus on the big scores that required more confidence and skill, I spent nearly the entire month of January reading finance and trading books. Surprisingly, none offered any detailed personal financial experiences. All the narratives were very general in nature and the detailed ones were entirely formulaic. These books were useful, but I wanted more.

Meanwhile, I watched the overall market continue its free fall with little resistance of any kind. This kind of price action made me even more confident that I was correct to focus on short selling. As much money as I had made short selling large companies, the market was simply too liquid and the stocks were priced too high for me to hold long enough and take positions large enough to make any really big money. I needed to focus on my bread-and-butter marketplace: the microcap niche. This market segment offered much less liquidity but significantly greater volatility. I prepared myself to return to this sector once more—this time from the short side.

Chapter 8: Margin of Safety

It's a commonly held belief that short selling microcap securities is particularly dangerous because their stock prices are so volatile. Maybe that's true, but I crave that volatility. I knew that my previous experience of playing this marketplace from the long side would help me navigate my way around the sector's land mines. My incredible profit history proved that microcaps, while dangerous, did in fact move with reason if you were intent on following the price action closely.

In the past, I'd bought momentum stocks during their run-ups, trying to sell near their peaks. Now, I looked for the same kinds of price patterns, but I planned on using these stocks' peaks as an entry point to take short positions. Even though the overall market was down, the stocks of tiny companies still managed a few spikes every now and then as their prices could still increase exponentially within a few days. It was almost like the good ol' days, but now I was much wiser. I'd been watching from the sidelines for nearly a month, but by early February 2002, I couldn't stand aside any longer. There were definitive breaking points during these stocks' price spikes, and I just needed to wait for the appropriate price action to occur before short selling into them.

A tiny technology company, LML Payment Systems (LMLP)(*t*), was my first play. Their stock price had risen from a few dollars per share to $70 back in 2000, but quickly fell back down to the single digits. Now, within a few days, it burst from $2 to the $6 price range, and the upside momentum appeared to be fading. Before shorting, I couldn't wait for the sideways price action to occur because the stock price might drop too quickly, stranding me on the sidelines. So, as usual, I broke my rules and gradually shorted the stock in the $6 price range. The good news was that the trading volume had already faded and I didn't bet very large.

I loved the plays with the fading trading volumes. I asked myself what kind of investors would buy a stock that had risen 300% in a few days. Not many people would, so what few buyers were present would become more hesitant to pull the trigger if the stock price began dropping. Short sellers would then sense a reversal and jump in. People who'd bought the stock before the run-up would want to lock in their profits by selling their shares. Ultimately, this type of trading should lead to a collapse in the stock price.

So, for a few days, I continued to hold my short position, comforted by the gradually falling stock price. One morning, LMLP
promptly dropped 50¢ to the $5 price range, so, within seconds,
I covered my entire position. After risking less than $120,000,
or approximately 20% of my capital, I wound up earning nearly
$22,000. This was a good omen for this new strategy

I patiently waited to exploit this pattern again, but unfortunately, it rarely occurred. The truth was that only a few companies were able to quickly spike 200 to 300% while the overall
market was still struggling to find its footing. Still, during the
first half of the year, I played variations of this pattern nearly a
dozen times and my gains were solid. Within a few months, I had
earned slightly over $250,000, as this strategy averaged nearly
$20,000 in profits per trade. I rarely bet more than $150,000 on
any one trade, but despite my success, I continued breaking my
trading rules. I continually held overnight and didn't wait for any
sideways price action before short selling.

Sometimes I even went back to short selling large companies that exhibited the same pattern and I still made money. I became so confident that I even began betting larger dollar amounts
in the $200,000 to $300,000 range, which represented rather
healthy chunks of my net worth. I figured this was acceptable
because my losses were minimal and my many large profits spoke
for themselves. But my chronic lack of discipline would come
back to bite me when the market environment wasn't as conducive
to short selling. At the height of my success, I'd sewn the seeds to
my demise as I'd done three years earlier by drilling holes into my
tennis rackets.

Now, I was so confident in my trading that I started a scholarship at Tulane. I wanted to encourage students and alumni who displayed unusual but not necessarily academic or athletic talents such as my talent for trading. Previously, whenever I'd enjoyed a string of profitable trades, I'd rewarded myself and my friends with fancy dinners, expensive bar tabs and elaborate parties, but this brought my spending into a whole new realm. My previous splurges had cost only a few hundred or sometimes a few thousand dollars at a time, but this scholarship cost $15,000. I put it on my AMEX card. I'd become infatuated with leaving something behind while also wanting to do something to help the credibility of the trading profession in general.

The vast majority of day traders lose money, and the media has been eager to convey the message that trading is nothing more than gambling. As a result, the trading profession has gotten a bad rap. One trader in particular became so frustrated with his losses that he burst into his trading office with guns blazing, murdering and injuring a dozen people before killing himself. Everybody remembers this incident, but nobody had heard about the many success stories. I hoped to do my part to change public perception with my scholarship.

I tried getting my longtime broker, E*Trade, to cosponsor my scholarship, but they'd fallen on hard times and told me they weren't interested. Maybe they'd researched my trading records that showed how I only made my huge profits by risking large percentages of my total capital and concluded that continued success seemed unlikely.

While I wanted to call it *The Timothy Sykes Award for Students Who Learn Good*, inspired by the movie *Zoolander*, Tulane nixed this amusing but grammatically incorrect name. I was forced to call it the rather awkward-sounding *Timothy Sykes Day Trading Award for the Talented,* but the objective of the award was still the same, and a university committee chose two students as the inaugural recipients of the award. One student had created a successful magazine from scratch, and the other was an up-and-coming film director.

In early May 2002, when I presented the award in front of a large audience, it was one of my proudest moments. This was my first inkling of how my story could help inspire others, but I was still too young and immature to explore this line of thinking any further.

Since it was rare for an undergraduate student to start a scholarship, I made a few local headlines. It even turned me into a sort of VIP around campus. This status allowed me to attend various university functions, socialize with the university big-shots and skip more classes—all of which helped to boost my already enormous ego. As much as I enjoyed my newfound local celebrity, I decided I needed a more worldly perspective. For the upcoming fall semester, I enrolled in the study-abroad program Semester at Sea, a traveling university that taught classes while sailing around the world for a little over three months. While aboard the ship, I doubted I'd be able to trade, but I figured I'd earned the right to take some time off. Even though my dedication to trading was unwavering, I wouldn't allow it to interfere with my international travel ambitions.

Meanwhile, I made plans for the future.

In the summer of 2002, I moved to New York City so I could dine at all the best restaurants, enjoy the nightlife and make connections for a potential career on Wall Street. Since I'd

just finished my junior year of college, few financial professionals took me seriously, considering me to be merely a lucky young
speculator. Maybe they were right. More importantly, I managed
to indulge myself at 80 of the city's best restaurants and had a
fine time.

In between my social life and endless networking, I continued to focus on trading. I knew it'd be difficult or maybe even
impossible to trade while onboard the ship in the fall, so I wanted to make as much money as I could before then. This attitude
was dangerous. I stupidly began trading stocks like Microsoft
and the Standard & Poor's depositary receipts (a stock that tracks
the Standard & Poor's [S&P] 500 Index) because there were few
worthy plays and I needed profits. Without any kind of trading plan, I had no business playing these stocks, but I couldn't
help myself. I lost over $50,000 in Microsoft and $20,000 in the
S&P depositary receipts, due mainly to my stubbornness to take
any small losses whatsoever. Luckily, I managed to profit from
several worthy short plays, and their resulting profits offset the
losses from my ego-based trading. Miraculously, I even managed
to earn an overall profit of nearly $50,000 for the summer. It was
yet another important lesson: *overtrading*, or excessive trading,
destroys your chances at reaching the very goal that drives you to
overtrade in the first place.

In the fall of 2002, I was pleasantly surprised that the
Semester at Sea ship boasted a satellite Internet connection,
enabling me to trade during our voyage. I was excited but also
somewhat scared; did I really want to risk betting hundreds of
thousands of dollars over a wireless satellite Internet connection?
After all, I was not very familiar with wireless connections at the

time and I didn't trust them. Besides, the time zone difference would make it difficult to watch the markets very closely. For the first half of our voyage, I stayed away from trading entirely.

Instead, I made the most of my time off and devoted my energy to making many new friends. It felt great to finally be able to hang out for hours on end and fit into the college social scene without worrying about the markets. I was so thrilled about my newfound social life that I felt compelled to be nice to just about everyone. This feeling was new to me, as I formerly had never had the patience to be very amiable. The only times I'd been so open and sociable were during my celebrations whenever I had made a ton of money. Of course, it was easy then. I liked being the center of attention.

But this was incredible. I couldn't believe how much happier I was when I didn't have to worry about trading. Maybe I subconsciously resented the profession because it prevented me from having a normal life. Was the money I made really worth the sacrifice? Maybe I just got along with this particular group of people extremely well and was looking into this too deeply. As intriguing as such self-analysis was, I didn't have much time to delve into it further. The pull of the markets was too strong. Mid-way through our voyage, I recognized that the market environment had become ripe with opportunities. I dove back in again.

The overall market dropped rather precipitously throughout the majority of 2002 but bounced decisively into late fall. The bounce was impressive, but the market's failure to break any important price levels to the upside led me to believe it was due for another drop. Similarly, the stock prices of many tiny technology companies had dropped, bounced and now appeared ready for a quick pullback. When these plays appeared on my watch lists, they were relatively easy prey for short sellers like me. One stock had tripled from $5, so I shorted it as it broke through the psychologically important $15 price barrier to the downside. I covered for more than $2 per share, or a quick $30,000 profit, in just over two hours. Forget about self-analysis. There was easy money to be made!

In order to get out of classes to trade, I went back to my high school days of pretending to be sick. It took some solid acting on my part, as everyone was so close together on the ship, but I pulled it off. I was right to stay put. I made another quick $30,000 on a stock that dropped nearly 20% intraday after it had quadrupled to $10 over the previous three days. This pattern seemed to work like clockwork even with the ship's unstable Internet connection. Every minute of satellite Internet access cost 50¢, but my profits from these two trades alone were already 30 times that of my eventual Internet bill. I quickly forgot about my trip altogether and readjusted my priorities to focus on trading once again.

Potential trades were materializing nearly every day now, but I was disciplined enough to ignore most of them. I was trading in less-than-ideal conditions, so I knew I couldn't participate in the trades that weren't absolutely perfect. I began thinking that this unstable environment might actually be good for me because it forced me to focus on the best plays.

Toward the end of the trip and during a violent storm, an incredible trading opportunity appeared. Throughout most of the summer, this stock languished in the $4 range but had rebound-

ed strongly over the previous three days to the $9 range on some-
what strong trading volume but without any news. It seemed like
its price strength was simply following the overall market, but now
the market had begun to roll over. This was a classic short selling setup pattern, especially since the trading volume on the stock
dropped significantly on the third day of the run-up. That was my
cue to start short selling.

At first, I started short selling the stock gradually, but because I expected a drop of $1 or maybe even $2 per share, I wanted to load up on my position to reap the greatest possible dollar
gain. But one afternoon, I became so confident in my position that
I built it up to 85,000 shares and in doing so, risked $700,000 of
my capital. This would be my largest gamble ever, which, ideally,
would lead to my largest profit ever. I held overnight, but thanks
to the great success I had enjoyed from this pattern many times
before, I wasn't very worried.

The next day, I awoke to see the stock price falling at the
market open, and I excitedly began buying to cover my short position to take my profits. But precisely when I had covered my first
5,000-share block for a gain of 75¢ per share, the ship's Internet
went off-line. I'd seen this happen a few times before, so I didn't
panic. I tried to relax and told myself that the Internet would be
back online within a few minutes. But after an incredibly tense
seven minutes, I started to panic. I felt beads of sweat forming on
my forehead, and my heart began pumping harder. Without being
able to cover my short position, I began envisioning the possibility
of the stock spiking and the losses I'd be forced to endure.

I raced to find a ship employee to see if there was anything
that could be done. After a few minutes, I found one and he suggested I use the satellite phone, as it rarely ever went down. OK,

I could still call my broker and he would execute my orders; this was acceptable. When I reached the phone station, my enthusiasm diminished as I found a line of four students in front of me. The students were apparently scared of the storm, so they wanted to call their parents for reassurance. This was ridiculous; the storm wasn't even bad enough to cancel classes! I raised my voice as I quickly explained my situation to everyone within earshot. The wild look in my eyes must've scared them even more than their fear of drowning because they agreed to let me cut the line to call my broker. Unfortunately, just as I reached the front of the line, another ship employee posted a sign saying the satellite phone was out of service for the time being. Damn!

I raced back to the computer room to find the Internet back online, but now all the computers were in use by other students. Once again, I quickly explained my situation and finally agreed to pay some kid $20 to use his computer. When I logged on, I discovered the stock price even lower and my profits even greater. The storm had actually helped make another $12,000 for me and I quickly covered the rest of my shares. I had taken profits totaling nearly $87,000 and I had an amazing trading story to tell.

After this near disaster, I wouldn't risk any further large amounts of money for the duration of the trip. I kept my trades small but still took additional profits totaling $40,000. Some of these trades occurred while we had lost all connections, but I was neither as worried nor as panicked because my positions were small and all the trade setups were perfect. While I lost many of my new friends because I started trading again, I was nearly $200,000 richer. It was unfortunate, but successful trading required total focus, and I was willing to make whatever sacrifices necessary.

Overall, I thoroughly enjoyed the trip and was glad I didn't let trading prevent me from this experience. We visited over a dozen developing countries, and the trip opened my eyes to worldwide poverty and cultural differences, which only made me appreciate my newfound wealth even more.

When I got back to the US, I was forced to change my strategy once again. Shares became more difficult to borrow because it now seemed like everybody wanted to be a short seller. After all, in order to take negative positions in stocks, short selling required the borrowing of shares, and the market's continued slump meant that short selling was the optimal trading strategy for the foreseeable future.

For the year, the overall market sustained heavy losses and it seemed like short sellers were the only ones making any money. I pocketed nearly $500,000—my second-best year since 2000. I was now a millionaire, even after taxes, and all before my 22nd birthday. I celebrated by buying biographies of famous business leaders. I wanted to learn how other people handled success so I could better manage mine.

My parents tried to make me slow down, but all I wanted to do was expand. I was cockier than ever. The fact that I had made so much money under less-than-ideal conditions led me to believe I was almost infallible. I should've taken a lesson from all the patterns I followed: nothing that rises so quickly can stay on top for very long.

I began the new year by short selling a variety of micro-cap plays that had all recently demonstrated exceptional price strength. For the first time, I spread my assets around, taking on multiple plays simultaneously, figuring I would either take small profits on some while averaging higher on the others or take small profits on all of them. My plan was nothing less than brilliant; there wasn't any doubt in my mind. The profits from my winners would be nice, but my losing positions would inevitably reverse in my favor sometime in the future, so I would be able to cover for profits if I could just stand the pain long enough. Incredibly, this strategy broke all my trading rules simultaneously, but I was determined to proceed nonetheless. I held for days or weeks at a time, refusing to take any losses whatsoever. My ego was in complete control and I wasn't interested in being conservative any longer. I had made my first million with seemingly little effort and on a part-time basis. What might I accomplish if I devoted all my time and energy to this profession?

I believed that if I really put my heart and soul into it, I could make $1 million in profits for 2003. As much as I wanted to achieve this goal, I also didn't want to risk any more of my new-found wealth than necessary. I decided to see if I could find other investors to add their capital to my operation, which would lessen my personal risk. I knew most fund managers simply took fees for managing other people's money, so, while still very different from that of other financial professionals, this strategy would bring me closer to the mainstream. I began asking everyone I knew if they knew anybody wealthy to join in my trading business. I had a phenomenal multi-year track record that had been produced during the most volatile market environment in history, so I didn't think it would be difficult to find investors. But I knew that having so little money under management hurt my status as a true market wizard, so I was determined to build my operation quickly.

One of my parents' friends was interested to hear about the strategies that had made me so much so quickly. He promised that if he liked what I had to say, he'd fund my operation to the tune of a few million dollars. My enthusiasm dwindled when he asked for all the details without giving me any assurances that he wouldn't simply use the strategies for himself. In addition, he wanted all my results to be fully audited. The fact that I had made approximately 100 times my initial investment within four years was just a little too unbelievable. After some careful thought, I declined his offer.

I needed time to consider all my options. I wanted my shot at the big time, but I wasn't sure how much I was willing to risk to get there. This was my first experience with the great financial paradox: how do you make investors give you money if you're not willing to disclose the process by which you intend to make them more money?

I called several other family friends who worked in the industry to see if they'd be interested in hiring me as a trader. If I was about to give away all my trading secrets, at least I wanted to have a salary to fall back on. While they listened politely to how I traded, they clearly had no idea what I was talking about. Along with 99.9% of the civilized world, they considered the microcap sector to be akin to gambling. It didn't help that there had never been any academic studies or books to support my theories. They declined the opportunity to allow me to try to prove myself.

Next, I thought about publishing my trading strategies and making money from the subsequent book royalties and seminar fees. My earnings probably wouldn't stretch into the millions, but the seminars would definitely be a cash cow and I would earn a decent living for years to come. Even though my message board experience taught me that the audience was out there, there was no guarantee that anyone would pay to listen to a kid like me. And it was the cowardly way out. I began to remember how guilty I felt when I ruined my first successful trading strategy by sharing it with too many people. Why make the same mistake again? Besides, my time was too valuable to waste on telling other people how to make money. I needed to find a way to become a true financial professional.

I began thinking about how I would really prefer to keep trading on my own. While I knew I could easily join a proprietary trading firm, or *prop firm*, which allowed people to trade their own money with the added ability to borrow capital and use tremendous leverage, I decided that that would only serve to increase my risk, not reduce it. As cocky as I was, I didn't want to take on any more risk. Instead, I'd need to go back to my original idea and take on other investors. This would increase the assets with which I traded but reduce my personal stake in the operation. I couldn't start a *mutual fund*—a fund that raised money from shareholders who invested as a group—because that industry's rules prevented short selling. No, I'd have to start a *hedge fund*, which was similar to a mutual fund in structure but it allowed me to undertake all sorts of alternative investment strategies, including short selling.

In late January 2003, I invested in a new computer system that would better facilitate the expansion of my operation. After all, I was aiming high, so I needed a truly professional setup. I spent nearly $4,000 on the fastest computer available and attached a custom-made three-screen monitor. Such monitors are commonplace nowadays, but back then, they looked very futuristic. I designated two screens solely for stock charts and quotes, while the other received a TV signal—for CNBC, of course. After I set up this monstrosity in the bedroom of my Tulane apartment, I took a moment to reflect on how far I'd come in such a short period. This new equipment represented a commitment to trading as my life's work. My drive to succeed would take me to the pinnacle of financial success. I was sure of it. My conservative parents thought differently and made me put $160,000 into a five-year CD so I wouldn't be able to use that money for trading.

No Business
Chapter 9: Like Hedge Business

By the beginning of February 2003, I'd already put the pieces in motion to create my own hedge fund. I'd read all about how this relatively new type of fund would revolutionize the financial industry due to its investment flexibility, so this was the exact kind of legal structure that I needed. I read extensively about the industry just to be sure that it suited my needs and after much consideration, I decided it was the perfect corporate vehicle to explore all kinds of investment strategies. After all, my childhood dream was to become a mutual fund manager, and hedge funds had become the new mutual funds, so technically, I was about to turn my dream into reality. I found a consulting firm that dealt specifically with startup hedge funds, and with their help I hired a lawyer, an accountant and tech support. The new support team comforted me, since they had helped many new funds raise capital. Now, all I needed was a solid name for my new company.

Should I call it *Timothy Sykes Capital* or use my initials to create *TKS Capital*? Most funds seemed to be named after their firm's principal and it would certainly be nice to have my name recognized within the industry. No, I didn't want to come off as the cocky kid that I was. I needed a classier name—something respectable. I searched through all of the Greek and Roman gods' names, and every one of them seemed to have already been taken. I turned to Latin, famous fictional characters, financial terms—still nothing. After a week of coming up empty, I was so fed up with searching that I gave up on the respect angle and focused on something that I really enjoyed: food. I settled on the name *Cilantro Fund*, since the spice was known for being somewhat atypical, similar to my niche trading strategy. It was unique; people would definitely remember my fund. Once I had the name, it took only a few weeks and $10,000 to get everything set up, and another month to get all the legal paperwork approved by all the necessary government organizations.

When I'd previously traded on behalf of friends and family, everyone made money, but I decided that setup just wasn't for me. Sure, they sent me gifts and treated me to dinners, but the money I had made for them greatly exceeded all the freebies. No, I wouldn't make that rookie mistake again. I was a professional trader now.

Hedge fund managers, on average, received a 20% cut of any fund profits, but my lawyer said that my lofty historical performance justified higher fees. He told me stories about how I'd eventually have more money than I'd know what to do with if I continued to churn out steady profits, and I believed him. I figured my strategies were worth it. In addition to the 2% annual management fee I would earn, whether I made money or not, I would take a 30% cut of the fund's profits. I scoffed at the 2% annual management fee, since it seemed to be a cowardly way of making money, but I liked that it would help offset the fund's expenses. In fact, I also considered any money market interest the fund would earn as insulting, too. Still, I begrudgingly agreed to the few thousand dollars in monthly interest as a kind of bonus for my short holding periods.

Unfortunately, I'd never created a business from scratch before, and the substantial paperwork and legal filings nearly overwhelmed me. After all, I'd stupidly initiated this whole process during my last, and most difficult, semester at Tulane. I probably should've waited until after graduation, but I wanted to start raising capital immediately to reduce the personal risk associated with my trading.

So, I pushed forward with the firm that had helped set up my fund. Upon their advice, I sucked up the $15,600 cost to audit my previous trades from 1999 to 2002, so that potential investors would see I wasn't exaggerating when I told them how well I had done. The audit also revealed how much I had actually traded in dollar terms throughout the years. I traded $2.6 million worth of stock in 1999, $73 million in 2000, $70 million in 2001 and $102 million in 2003. Those were some hefty numbers! For the first time, I realized just how razor thin my profit margins were—they were pathetic!

Still, on a percentage basis, I had produced the highest average annual return over the previous few years of anybody in the hedge fund industry. Funds reported profits in percentage terms and adjusted the percentages to account for fund fees—meaning, my 30% cut of any profits and my 2% annual management fee. According to my audit, I had earned 910% in 1999, 560% in 2000, 47% in 2001 and 98% in 2002, for a ridiculous average annual return of 323%. Adjusted to account for fund fees, I had earned 564.91% in 1999, 292.64% in 2000, 35.08% in 2001 and 86.89% in 2002, for a still outstanding average annual return of 244.88%. By all accounts, nobody even came close to my official performance, so I thought it would be a cinch to raise a few million dollars. I really began to believe that I had a distinct advantage over all other funds. At the very least, my numbers should get me some attention, and then it would be up to me to continue the streak. While I'd learn the realities of the hedge fund industry soon enough, for the moment, I truly believed the sky was the limit.

Once I'd calculated all my returns, I immediately began contacting everyone I'd ever met to see if they or somebody they knew would be interested in investing in my fund. To display my results for all to see, it seemed only natural to also create a corporate website, but my lawyer squashed that idea very quickly.

He explained that industry regulations prohibited hedge funds from any publicity, talking to the press, soliciting random investors, placing advertisements, being listed in the Yellow Pages or having any websites for public viewing. Instead, industry websites were required to be password protected and funds were required to have pre-existing relationships with any investors they approached. Basically, hedge funds weren't to have any contact with industry outsiders unless the outsiders were extremely wealthy—meaning, they were *accredited investors*. The SEC defined accredited investors to be anyone who was worth at least $1 million or had made $200,000 in each of the past two years. This limitation was created to protect non-wealthy investors from investing in hedge funds due to the high risks associated with our investment strategies. After all, the minimum investment in most hedge funds was $250,000—or even $1 million. There was simply no room for non-wealthy people so why should they be allowed to hear any of the details. The SEC felt it was their duty to protect non-accredited investors from their own greed, and the agency clearly didn't trust hedge fund managers to reject unworthy investors.

I was shocked. Sure, I'd read about the restrictions placed on hedge funds before, but I didn't understand to what extent. After all, business was business. America was a nation founded on a free market economy and the right to freedom of speech. These regulations ran counter to everything America stood for. What kind of an industry had I gotten myself into? As frustrating as these ridiculous rules were, I was new to the industry, so I wasn't in any position to start fighting with the government body that regulated it. If I wanted any kind of future as a hedge fund manager, I'd have to submit to the SEC's tyranny. I didn't bother creating any password-protected website because it simply wouldn't have been cost-effective for me at this point. As for pre-existing relationships, I knew only a few wealthy people through family connections, but how tough could it really be to find people who wanted to make average annual returns of 200%? It was just a matter of time before the investors would start rolling in.

Meanwhile, my strategy of spreading my short positions around was actually working quite beautifully. Within the first two months of the year, I had taken nearly $100,000 in total profits. I was ecstatic because, once again, I was on track for a million-dollar year, even if it was really too early to tell. Unfortunately, these profits hid the ugly truth behind their creation: I was still breaking my trading rules. I was short selling into these momentum stocks and increasing my positions as their prices surged higher, betting that I could cover my shorts when their prices reversed to the downside. This had always worked well in the past, but then again, I'd usually taken only one or two positions at a time. Now I was taking several positions simultaneously, and my risk increased dramatically.

My losses hadn't been very large on any one position yet, but I was risking greater amounts of capital over longer time periods in less than ideal plays. While I knew these plays were second-rate, the lack of worthy opportunities wouldn't prevent me from trading! I would stop at nothing to achieve my goal of having a million-dollar year. I simply didn't have the patience to wait for more-solid plays. As long as I was making money, what did it matter anyway?

I found out soon enough.

I discovered a waste management company, Clean Harbors (CLHB)(*t*), that seemed to be a potentially worthy short selling opportunity. In less than a year, their stock price had risen from the $4 to the $18 range but by early 2003 had dropped to $12 per share. The company was involved in a rather complex merger that forced them to announce—just two weeks before the deadline— that they wouldn't be able to file their quarterly report with the

SEC on time. On this news, their stock price quickly dropped from $12 to $9 as investors panicked. I'd seen stocks completely collapse on news like this before, so I figured any bounce would be a great short selling opportunity. Within a day, the stock bounced to $10, and I opened my short position. The price continued to bounce higher, so I stayed true to my recent strategy, averaging my cost basis higher by adding to my short position. Within a few days, my position had grown to over 70,000 shares, or nearly three-quarters of my entire net worth. Hours upon hours of research led me to believe that there was a high probability of additional negative news forthcoming. Any further negative news would surely drop the stock to the $6 price range, which would yield nearly $250,000 in profits for me.

But I was living in a dream world.

I'd never based a short position—let alone my largest position ever—purely on fundamental research, but now my ego had taken complete control once again. I was incredibly sure my gamble was right on. CLHB dipped for a few hours, and I could've covered my short position with a small profit, but instead I increased my position, precisely when the stock price spiked against me. Even as the stock price rose, I was so sure I was right that I held firm. But after two days of further price strength, I couldn't stand the pain any longer and I covered my entire short position for a $120,000 loss. I was humiliated. I had put myself in a position where I had risked too much capital—all based entirely on a hunch. I had now lost money trading on the year for the first time in my life.

What had just happened? While this was only a 10% hit to my total net worth, I just couldn't believe that I had made such a horrible trade and, worse, taken such a large position. The stock had rightfully pummeled me and there was nothing I could do about it. For the next few days, I took it so personally that I continued to watch the stock like a hawk, ignoring past lessons by becoming obsessed with making my money back. I truly believed CLHB would soon plunge and I wanted to be there when it happened.

When the stock broke an important level to the downside, I pounced. I was determined to show the stock who was boss. I re-shorted with the full force of my entire account, building a million-dollar position within a few hours. In my excitement, I barely recognized that my position was nearly half of the stock's daily trading volume and that I had only $900,000 of cash in my account. I was $100,000 over the limit, so I was using margin for the first time in my life. But I was determined to do whatever it would take to make back my loss and more. Unfortunately, once again, the stock price moved against me from the start and I was forced to cover my short for another huge loss.

This time around, I had lost $130,000. What little confidence I had after my last loss was now completely shattered, and my hedge fund was only days away from going live. Now I really felt like an idiot. I wouldn't have been nearly as angry if the loss had occurred on a worthy play, but this wasn't close to being anywhere near worthy. I'd become too emotionally involved and ignored what the price action was trying to tell me. Now I had paid the price. Before CLHB, I had been up $100,000 on the year. Now I was down more than $150,000.

Four years later, the merger turned out to be a complete success, as CLHB now trades in the $50 range. I was just dead wrong. It was a rather expensive lesson, but it helped me realize how easily everything could fall apart when I ignored the price action.

This $350,000 turnaround was definitely an inauspicious way for
me to start my hedge fund. I'd planned on starting with an even
$1 million in total assets—$900,000 from my own accounts and
$100,000 from my parents—but instead, my fund now started
with a measly $650,000. I thought about calling back into service
the $160,000 I'd set aside in the CD only a few weeks earlier but
wisely did not.

On top of my capital problem, one of my brand-new computer monitors broke, and I couldn't replace it unless I sent back
the entire computer system. I couldn't afford the downtime, so I
sucked it up and promised to fix it when things cooled down. I
was now trying to balance my schoolwork and trading with meetings with potential investors. The pressure to perform to impress
investors led me to open positions in several more second-rate
trades, and I lost nearly 4% in my first month in operation as a
hedge fund.

Even though I wanted to focus solely on trading, I knew I
had to start networking to raise capital. Ideally, I wanted to sched-
ule meetings after the market close, but as I began making the
rounds, everybody seemed to prefer lunchtime meetings. I foolishly scheduled several of these intraday meetings and this hurt
my performance even more because now I missed the few worthy
plays out there entirely. It taught me yet another valuable lesson:
nothing can interfere with trading during market hours. I had my
own money to worry about, so as much as I wanted to build my
fund, I could no longer afford to put potential investors ahead of
my current investors—namely, me and my parents. I rededicated
myself to finding the strongest plays possible. As a result, I sacri-
ficed much of my social life during the last few months of college.

My obsession with positive performance grew so strong that I even missed my college graduation ceremony. My parents and grandparents, who'd come down from Connecticut, weren't very pleased, but their anger subsided after I informed them that I had made nearly $18,000 on the trade that had detained me. They told me how proud they were that I understood that great sacrifice was sometimes necessary. This unwavering devotion to trading had helped me earn nearly 2% during my second month in operation as a hedge fund. That monthly gain, while small, helped to restore the confidence needed to push forward with my fund.

For the time being, I decided to stay in New Orleans because I didn't want a big move to interfere with my trading. Also, I still had many potential New Orleans–based investors to meet with. Now I made sure to meet with them only after the market close or on weekends. Even after I explained my reasoning, many couldn't understand, so I let them fall by the wayside. They could never understand how much focus was required in trading. I knew I wouldn't remain in New Orleans for very long, but I'd worry about moving only after I had made back all the money I had recently lost.

The day after graduation, one of my closest childhood friends told me he'd found somebody interested in my fund. What's more, his contact was supposedly worth tens of millions of dollars because he was the chief financial officer (CFO) of some major financial firm in south Florida. He wanted to meet me so I could explain my strategy in person. I was struggling to find wealthy connections, so I jumped at this opportunity, driving eight hours from New Orleans to the investor's home in Florida.

When I arrived, I found him and his buddy drinking beer and hitting golf balls on the course behind his home. They were very friendly, so we hung out for a few hours before getting down to business around dinnertime.

I pitched them for nearly two hours and was pleased that they actually seemed to understand how I had made money. I really thought I had a shot at raising capital until they informed me that they preferred mutual funds due to their low risk. Damn! Why'd they even bring me out here in the first place? One of them went so far as to suggest that I should close up shop, find a more scalable and less volatile strategy, and live off the management fees. The thought of living off fees alone disgusted me. No, I wouldn't even consider it; I was a trader, not a traitor. I tried to explain that I hadn't chosen this strategy; its consistent profits had basically chosen me. My explanation didn't change their minds, so I drove back to New Orleans and sulked. At least I'd practiced my pitch and received another lesson: no matter your performance; if you want to raise capital, you must market yourself effectively.

For nearly two weeks after graduation, I remained in New Orleans, trading by day and meeting with potential investors by night. Trading was somewhat slow, and only some of the people I met were actually interested in investing with me. Many were uncomfortable with investing in a speculative operation. Clearly, the big money lay elsewhere. I began searching for additional capital by building a list of contacts in the startup hedge fund world. After the list topped out at 100 people, I e-mailed and called everybody for advice. My e-mails were very general in nature as I was more paranoid than ever about industry regulations.

Many of these people were somewhat helpful in explaining this industry to me, while others simply referred me to their contacts. One such referral created an e-mail debate between a business journalist and me.

Within days, our e-mail conversation was published on *CBS Marketwatch* and gave me some much needed exposure. The article summarized my trading strategies but argued my high returns wouldn't last. Its slightly negative tone made me more determined than ever to prove the author wrong. While the publicity helped me expand my contact list, the only additions were traders and investors who wanted to know more about my strategy's details for their personal exploitation. I still had a ways to go before I raised any serious capital, so I kept networking and talking to anybody who would listen. Some people were more helpful than others, but everybody gave me at least one contact that in turn helped deepen my understanding of this mysterious industry.

As my search for capital continued, I discovered that one of the detrimental effects of industry regulations was the difficulty in differentiating between people who told the truth and those who didn't. Since I couldn't find much information on these firms on my own, I didn't know whom to believe. Some people claimed to have big money; others claimed big money connections; and mostly everyone was out for themselves and wouldn't trust an industry outsider like me. Clearly, I wouldn't see any money until I could gain people's trust, and that meant meeting them in person. The epicenter of the hedge fund industry was New York City, so, to grow my fund, I decided to move there.

The competition would be tough, but that's where the money was. Also, if I planned to dominate this industry, I'd better understand it, and people weren't talking details to somebody claiming to have a small fund based in New Orleans.

Before my move, I visited New York City for a week to meet with some of the contacts I'd only talked to over the phone. After meeting with them, I had a better understanding of the industry, but none of them said they could help me until I was much more established. Perfect: I needed their help now, not later. Nonetheless, I kept their contact information and made sure to call on them again in the future.

Meanwhile, I used this trip to go apartment hunting. After seeing several seemingly overpriced places, I found a reasonably priced SoHo loft. It was large enough to comfortably live and work in, saving me the combined cost of an apartment and an office. Of course, the monthly rent was still $3,200, nearly 10 times that of my New Orleans rent. But I went for it anyway. If I was going to be big-time, this expense would be a drop in the bucket.

In late May 2003, I completed my move to New York City. My lawyer disagreed with the move because he thought I'd only incur additional costs. He claimed that based on my performance, I'd eventually find investors and that it was best to have patience and keep the overhead low. While he represented several funds that surged from a few million dollars to tens of millions in assets, he didn't understand my trading strategies. Experience taught me that consistently profitable strategies came and went without warning, so I needed to grow my capital base quickly to take full advantage of them.

I decided to pay the $12,000 annual fee for a premium listing on *Hedgefund.net*—the largest online hedge fund database—to publish all my fund information. While this was a large expense for a fund my size, it was the only form of SEC-compliant advertising available, so I considered it crucial to my success. And it would be completely worthwhile if I found just one or two investors from the site. I also posted my returns on several other free hedge fund databases, but I put little faith in those; after all, you get what you pay for. My lack of patience pressed me further to look for outside professionals to help raise capital. Thus began my education of *third-party marketing firms*.

Third-party marketing firms raise capital for hedge funds in exchange for a piece of the action. They get paid by taking lump-sum payments, varying percentages from the fees earned on any capital they help raise or a combination of the two. Within my first two months of operation as a hedge fund, I contacted nearly four dozen of these firms, but I couldn't find a fit. Some wanted large up-front lump-sum payments ranging from $5,000 to $35,000, while others demanded monthly fees anywhere from $2,000 to $15,000. Some could live with taking a percentage of the management and incentive fees on any capital they helped raise, but their cuts would wipe out nearly half of my potential profits. Of course, nobody could guarantee that they could even raise capital for me; I'd just have to trust in their abilities and contacts.

In addition, I'd have to use the brokers with whom the third-party marketing firms were affiliated because they received additional commissions on assets they'd steer their way. And these were the stipulations of the firms that wanted to work with me. The vast majority of third-party marketing firms declined to represent me for a whole list of reasons: my returns were too good to last, my present asset base was too small, my market niche was too narrow, I took too few trading positions, investors didn't respond to one-man shops and my strategy was too difficult to market. Blah, blah, blah.

The one marketer who appeared the most interested in representing my fund wanted to focus on basic marketing: PowerPoint presentations and logo design. He just happened to know somebody who'd designed the logo of several Fortune 500 firms, so he could engineer a deal for me to buy a top-notch logo for only $15,000. I wondered what his cut would be. What a joke. I either had to play ball with all these ridiculous stipulations or not be allowed into the game. It was a tough lesson for a cocky kid like me, but these third-party marketing firms didn't seem right for my fund. I'd have to raise money on my own.

Thankfully, many of these firms referred me to their contacts and broker friends who were also in the capital-raising business. At first, I couldn't understand why they'd help me if they didn't represent me, but I began realizing that this business was based on contacts and referrals. OK, I could play that game.

I began visiting dozens of brokerage firms, all of which were recommended to me by my newfound industry contacts. I learned that in addition to providing trade execution services, they also promised to introduce capital to their clients, hoping for increased business in the form of higher commission volume. I'd always used basic online discount brokerages—E*Trade and Suretrade—so I was somewhat intimidated by these brokers' big promises, fancy offices and fees. I was still too small a fund to use the largest and most reputable firms, so I met with *IBs*, or introducing brokers. These smaller brokers had cut deals with the big boys to offer some of their services at discount prices to small hedge fund managers like me.

I needed to find a broker immediately to get my commissions and hopefully their capital-raising efforts on track. Since I
was short on time, I decided to try out six firms, opening accounts with all of them. Instead of the commissions of $10 per
trade I'd always paid, these firm's commissions ranged from a
half penny to two pennies per share traded. If I traded only a few
plays, this was chump change. Of course, if I fell into my habit of
overtrading, my commissions could really add up.

After a few weeks, I'd narrowed the list down to two
brokers. They promised the most help with capital introduc-
tions, and their commissions were under a penny per share. Even
though neither broker had tried to woo me with dinners like the
others had nor did either one have any online trading software,
I was still optimistic. One promised me that their online trading software would be ready within two weeks, but as a veteran
online trader, I figured this rigid setup would slow me down
considerably—just as it had on the Semester at Sea ship. I had
made a great deal of money when that setup prevented me from
overtrading, so maybe it would help again.

The other firm made some big promises but never came
through on any of them. The firm introduced me to private
investments in public equities (*PIPEs*) and special purpose acquisition companies (*SPACs*). PIPEs referred to deals in which
institutions invested in struggling publicly-traded companies
at discount market prices. SPACs were companies created for
the sole purpose of raising money to acquire other companies
at some later date. I didn't participate in either scheme because
these complex investments were far outside my comfort area. On
the trading side, this firm gave me the worst order executions I'd
ever seen, and they never delivered their online trading software

as promised. I was about to close my account with them to focus on the one quality broker I'd found, but I got sidetracked by an incredible-looking play.

During the last few days of May 2003, I put my broker problems on hold because there was some seemingly easy money to be made. Smith Micro Software (SMSI)(*t*) was just a lowly technology stock trading in the 50¢ price range when several newsletters decided to get together and send out buy alerts to millions of people via fax and e-mail. Several boiler rooms probably joined in the fun too, and the stock price nearly quadrupled to $2 within two days of the price-pumping.

I was disciplined enough to wait for the sideways price action before loading up. When it occurred, I shorted nearly 120,000 shares. I figured this would be an easy $40,000 profit, fully expecting the stock price to fade right alongside the trading volume once the price-pumping ended. I was partially correct, as the stock price did indeed fall, giving me paper profits of nearly $25,000, but I didn't take them because I wanted to get to my goal of $40,000. The trading volume faded perfectly, but the stock price just didn't seem to want to crack, and my gain stalled. You'd think I would've learned to take a profit by now, but you'd be wrong. Greedily, I hung in there.

I'd seen this pattern many times before and I figured I could get to the $40,000 profit mark if I just bided my time. Unfortunately, the next day, several more newsletters joined the price-pumping bandwagon, the stock price spiked and my entire profit was wiped out within a few hours. Multiple waves of price-pumping were commonplace, but the key was to realize when this was happening and exit any short position if the stock price was close to breaking out to new highs. But many shorts like me were stubborn and refused to cover. The heat of the action and the lack of solid business fundamentals in these plays often caused us to ignore the time-honored lesson: hype can make lesser companies rise faster than quality companies.

I was so cocky that I went so far as to add to my short position. Even though the stock's price action suggested higher prices ahead, I was sure that this company didn't deserve to trade at these elevated prices. But later in the day, the market proved me wrong and I surrendered, placing a limit order to cover my entire short position and take a $30,000 loss because the stock price appeared to be headed higher.

I waited for my execution to confirm my loss. My broker usually called back within a few seconds, but after nearly five minutes, my phone still hadn't rung. I frantically called them to hear that they'd executed only a very small portion of my order and that the rapidly rising stock price had already surged past my limit. I'd played this game several times before. I had to protect myself from a larger loss, so, to ensure execution, I put in a new limit that was much higher than the current stock price.

The stock price continued higher, and three minutes later, I called my broker once again. They had executed only half of my new order! This time I flipped out because this was entirely unacceptable. I now asked them to buy at market prices to get me out immediately. They did, and my total loss was $120,000. This was a catastrophe. Not only did it ruin my confidence—this being my third straight $100,000-plus loss in as many months—but it killed any hope of raising capital from outside investors anytime soon. My fund was now down 18% in May alone and 21% since the fund's March inception on assets of $660,000.

My mistakes were certainly piling up quickly. I had blown several trades and lost a great deal of money, so my ability to raise capital was compromised. I had to decide what to do about my brokers. Many people would've taken this chance to quit, but I chose to lick my wounds and learn from these experiences to get back into my trading groove. I was determined to return to my original strategy of taking quick profits and not risk getting trapped in short squeezes with oversized positions.

I transferred most of my remaining fund assets to my one quality broker, but I still traded small amounts with the broker who had such poor order executions. Why? Because, as terrible as their order executions were, I knew I could use their unrivaled ability to find borrowable shares of the stocks I wanted to short. On my target plays, I could make 50¢ to $1 per share, so a few pennies in execution slippage weren't so bad. I just needed to make sure never to risk getting caught in a short squeeze with them.

Shares had become somewhat difficult to borrow, since everybody now wanted to play the short selling game. It pained me to think about how much money I could've saved if this broker hadn't taken advantage of me, but I chalked it up to yet another expensive lesson: If you want proper order executions, enter the orders yourself. I couldn't even muster enough strength to yell at them, because they were only doing what shady financial firms had done for decades. I had no proof, but I could almost guarantee their traders bought positions for themselves before buying to cover my short position. In doing so, they bought at lower prices because they knew my massive buy orders would push prices higher and they could sell their shares for a profit. This practice was known as *front running* and was common at less reputable brokerage firms. It was my fault for giving them the opportunity to do this to me.

To prevent the possibility of any further losses, I cancelled my upcoming meetings with potential investors and stopped trading for the rest of the month. Hedge funds are graded monthly, so as dreadful as an 18% down month was, it wasn't necessarily a fund killer. However, anything worse definitely would've put me out of business. I turned to living it up in New York City, with my goal being to return to trading with a clear head in June.

During my mini-vacation, I tried not to think about trading, but I couldn't stay away completely. No matter how many parties, restaurants and nightclubs I went to or how hungover I felt the next day, I was still addicted to checking the markets. So, I redirected my efforts to finding better brokers. This time around, I wasn't rushed for time, so I could afford to be picky. After two weeks of continuous face-to-face meetings, I finally found a firm that appeared to meet my criteria. They told me they'd help me raise capital; find me the best *locates*, or borrowable shares of the stocks I wanted to short; and give me a complete online trading system with commissions costing me less than a penny per share. What else could I ask for? I was immediately hooked, so after testing their online trading software and seeing how good their locates really were, I closed my other accounts and transferred all my assets to this new broker. My two-week break from trading had been successful in clearing my head, so I was well prepared for the onslaught of upcoming trading opportunities.

The bear market had now turned into a bull market, and several stocks with gradually uptrending prices seemed ready to explode. All in all, it wasn't the best time to be a startup fund that focused on short selling, but that's the hand the market had dealt me.

By early June 2003, nearly a dozen microcap plays had risen exponentially within a few days. No industry was spared, as stocks like Oxigene (OXGN)(*t*), a biotech play, surged from $4 to $18; Qiao Xing (XING)(*t*), a Chinese technology play, climbed from $6 to $14; and VA Software (LNUX)(*t*), a software play, rose from $1 to $2.50—all on heavy trading volume. And these were just a few of them. My recent vacation helped me have more patience, so I bided my time, waiting for the right price action to occur before taking any short positions.

Within a few days of each other, I pounced on all three plays. The SMSI trade had taught me to take profits quickly in this newly bullish environment, so I shorted into these plays with low expectations. Within hours, I covered my short positions as they each dropped more than 20% off their intraday highs. I earned nearly 50¢ per share on LNUX, $2 per share on XING and $3 per share on OXGN. I didn't care how their stocks acted afterward because there was always something new to play. For the month of June, my fund earned over $60,000, or just over 9%, on assets of $723,000. While I was definitely excited, I was still far behind on the year. Luckily, these price spikes paled in comparison to July's market action.

Due to my recent money troubles, I was forced to take on a roommate for my SoHo loft in late June. While his contribution to the rent wasn't significant, it eased my anxiety about my overhead in general. It's difficult to stay focused on trading when you have to worry about your monthly expenses. As it turned out, he wanted to be a trader too, so we got along well. He traded a small personal account, but his passion for making money reminded me of myself and inspired me to work harder.

I knew that I wouldn't even begin to be taken seriously until I broke the psychologically important $1-million asset mark. After all, data suggested the average hedge fund had $50 million in assets, so my fund was just a drop in the bucket. Even though I had a long way to go, I was encouraged by my research that showed hedge funds could surge from a few million dollars to the $10-million to $20-million asset range within a few months. I needed to focus on posting returns that would spark investor interest. My daily market scans alerted me to two other stocks that I had played in June. These Asian plays had spiked even higher and now seemed like great potential shorts.

China Natural Resources (CHNR)(*t*) and Internet Initiative Japan (IIJI)(*t*) each had risen from $2 to $5 in June but hadn't come off their highs like every other recent play. I had taken small losses in these two stubborn stocks before, but now their elevated stock prices created opportunity. First, IIJI spiked from $5 to $14 in three days on increasingly heavy trading volume but without any news. The average daily trading volume had been a few hundred thousand shares, but now it spiked to nearly 15 million shares. Nobody knew why this particular stock rose so much, but nearly every Asian play was hot, and traders would play the momentum for as long as it lasted. Personally, I thought the stock price might collapse at any moment, but I wisely stayed on the sidelines until the price action confirmed a trend break.

On the fourth day of the run-up, the sideways price action cracked slightly and I immediately shorted 30,000 shares, or $400,000 worth of stock. My roommate jumped in with his own account and shorted 1,000 shares. We agreed that the stock price should collapse within minutes, but instead it held firm for nearly an hour. My nervousness forced me to cover some of my short position, while my roommate held his ground because he couldn't afford to jump in and out like me. The stock finally broke through another important price level, so I added to my short position on the way down. Two hours later, I covered my short for an $80,000 gain, while my roommate made $2,000. After being down 20%, my fund was now nearly breakeven for the year.

It was a time for celebration. I bought two ridiculously overpriced bottles of champagne at our favorite nightclub and partied until dawn with a mix of potential investors, friends and models. It was a great night.

As hungover as I was the next day, I still awoke before 8 a.m. to watch the market action. I knew that IIJI could easily bounce and provide a solid entry price to open another short position. And CHNR could follow IIJI's lead and also become a nice breakout play. I was right on both counts. By the end of the day, CHNR's stock price had jumped from $5 to $9. I resurrected my old gap-up strategy, buying near the market close and holding my position overnight. I was too scared to take a large position because I still thought the situation too risky. I had to protect my monthly performance. However, the stock price gapped higher to $11 and I took a few thousand dollars more in profits. I also managed to buy IIJI for a quick intraday bounce to make another $10,000 in profits.

My fund was now exactly breakeven since inception, but I began drooling at the prospect of actually going positive on the year. To do that, I continued to watch CHNR, planning to short the stock when the time was right. At $13, the trading volume faded and I thought the stock price could go no higher, so I shorted $130,000 worth of shares. I would've shorted more, but this stock was much less liquid than IIJI, so I couldn't risk getting caught in any potential short squeeze. The trading volume faded even more, and CHNR's counterpart, IIJI, quickly dropped to the single digits, so I looked forward to a similar downward price move in CHNR. Unfortunately, I hadn't waited for the important sideways price action, so the stock squeezed shorts like me during one afternoon. I was forced to cover at $15 for a $20,000 loss. As usual, I'd been too hungry for profits.

CHNR finally peaked at $16 and I re-shorted once the sideways price action cracked to the downside. I covered for a $20,000 gain that got me right back to breakeven. For July 2003, my fund gained over 14% on assets of $938,000, making me the top performer—on a percentage basis—in the industry. It was an exciting but bittersweet moment because I knew I could've done better.

New York City was expensive, but its high prices only inspired me to work harder to be able to afford everything. I'd never lived in a place where there was something interesting to do literally every single night of the week. Whether it was a new restaurant, art gallery, bar or nightclub opening, it didn't matter. My friends and I flocked to whatever was hot for networking and for hitting on beautiful women. I began going out almost every night. While I hadn't made any huge money lately, my reserves and my confidence in my trading abilities allowed me to spend nearly $1,000 weekly on socializing. I made myself and my fund known to everyone I could.

But industry regulations required any potential investors to certify in writing they were accredited before I could tell them any details about my fund. Many fund managers blatantly broke this rule, but I didn't want to risk any legal trouble. While some people followed through to find out more about my fund, this awkward step made my business seem complex and dangerous to new investors, scaring many of them away. My recent returns were positive, if not outstanding, so I persevered and continued making connections in the hope that my fundraising luck would soon change.

I became obsessed with the idea that the perception of wealth and success attracts investors. I was spending too much money on entertaining potential clients—other businesspeople and lower-end celebrities—but these relationships hadn't translated into any new investments yet. Only some of the people certified they were accredited investors, and many pretended to be interested in my business to keep the champagne flowing. I was frustrated, but this is how I knew financial firms had wooed customers for decades, so I played the game. I was learning the ropes of life in New York City's fast lane. It was fun but wearisome.

The good news was that my recent performance had finally convinced some family members and friends—the only accredited investors I knew—to invest in my fund. Earlier, they'd been scared away by the volatility of my returns, but my recent performance proved my trading strategies could still be hugely profitable. In August 2003, my fund broke through the million-dollar asset mark, just as a whole new set of trading opportunities arrived on the scene.

One energy company, Blue Dolphin Energy (BDCO)(*t*), skyrocketed from $1 to $4 in four days, while another tiny nutrition company, Nutrition 21 (NXXI)(*t*), surged from 50¢ to over $2 intraday. Instead of short selling right away, I patiently waited for the proper price action to occur in both stocks. When it did, I shorted BDCO at $3.50 and covered my short at $2.75 for a quick $35,000 gain. I made over $40,000 on NXXI by short selling the stock as it broke through several important price levels to the downside. On top of that, I was able to take larger positions because the daily trading volume surged to over 20 million shares.

Simply put, the market was incredibly liquid and volatile and I loved every second of it! Several smaller plays also contributed to $90,000 in earnings for September, which put my fund up a solid 10% for the year on assets of $1.1 million. Of course, when I finally reached 10%, I wanted to be up 15% or 20%; I was never satisfied. Ambition is an admirable trait for people in most industries, but it's dangerous for traders.

Within days of posting my September results on the hedge fund databases, several investors began calling me. For the first time in what seemed to be a very long time, I allowed myself to think about fundraising again. I had recently made some decent gains, but my networking activities were expensive. If I wanted to keep going out in search of contacts, I couldn't afford to lose any more capital. Even though I wanted to shoot for the big time, I had become somewhat conservative. Now I only risked up to 25%

of my fund's assets on any one position. I figured that if I could grow my fund to the $5-million to $10-million asset range, I would then be able to play with $500,000 positions once again, but with much less risk. If my trading worked well on that level, then I could aim for $25-million to $50-million and then maybe even more. One step at a time.

I was still a very tiny player in this marketplace. The daily trading volume on these plays frequently reached 10 million shares, while I traded only 10,000 to 30,000 shares at a time. It had become somewhat difficult to find borrowable shares, but there were still usually over 100,000 shares available to short on any given day. So, it would be a long time before my fund grew large enough for me to outgrow this niche. When that happened, I'd look for exploitable patterns elsewhere. It was all about being adaptable to rapidly changing market conditions.

All this thinking about my recent gains, the potential for greater gains and raising great amounts of capital combined to strengthen my determination to succeed. While coming back from being down 20% to having a positive yearly return felt great, it wasn't very remarkable in a bull market. Year-to-date, the market was now up nearly 20%, so investors would only be attracted to funds that outperformed that figure. In this environment, the funds that raised the most capital were the ones that produced 30%, 40% and 60% annual returns for their investors. My fund still had a great deal of catching up to do.

So, I tried to create trading opportunities when none existed. These plays were somewhat hit-or-miss, as their price action was far from perfect. I knew I shouldn't play them, but my yearning for profits overpowered reason. In the end, these plays were directly responsible for nearly $50,000 in losses, or a 6% loss for the fund, on assets of $1.03 million in October. The calls from investors stopped as quickly as they had begun. The industry didn't take kindly to large monthly losses, so it was yet another black mark on my record.

By the end of the year, I was completely disgusted with my performance. My fund finished 2003 with a measly 6.06% gain, net of fees, on assets of $1.06 million. The S&P 500, the most popular stock index with which most funds compared their returns, returned 28.69% for the year. For all my trading, worrying and risk taking, my fund had gotten crushed by a conservative index.

After each large gain since the beginning of the year, something inside my head snapped and made me aim for more gains. If I'd been patient enough to focus only on plays with worthy price action, they would've yielded an annual return in the neighborhood of 40%. The hit-or-miss plays that I had traded in the fall had prevented me from achieving the large overall returns I knew my strategy could yield. Many traders look back and regret the trades they missed; I look back and regret the trades I chose to play. With this discipline problem, I could still earn a decent living, but I wouldn't raise much outside capital.

Another disadvantage was that I was a one-man shop. Many other funds had grown exponentially through the efforts of several employees with decades of experience, wealthy connections and third-party marketing firms. I was just one young trader without any marketing firm or wealthy connections. The only thing I had going for me was my trading—I needed to focus on that.

I began thinking that while New York City was fun and promising, it hurt my trading. The overwhelming pressure I felt to succeed there made me overtrade in an attempt to prove myself as quickly as possible. Ironically, the outcome of these ill-advised plays defeated their very purpose. This line of thought brought me back to my experience in the summer of 2002 before I was about to go on Semester at Sea when my constant desire for profits was my undoing. Now, many of my trades were based on pure greed and I disregarded everything I'd learned about trading. My dream of growing my fund into a multi-million-dollar operation had all but faded as reality set in. Something needed to change.

Chapter 10: 2004: A Hedge Fund Odyssey

Maybe if I lived elsewhere, I wouldn't be reminded of all the tremendous opportunity the industry had to offer. Only then might I be able to focus solely on trading worthy opportunities instead of trying to will them into existence. I needed to forget about the hedge fund industry at large, stop spending money and put aside the daunting task of raising additional capital to get back to the basics of trading. I could still manage my fund, but my priorities needed to change. I loved the trading game for its purity, but I'd been sidetracked by everything that came with being a successful trader. I knew I needed to tune everything else out and return to the time when I was just a teenager who loved trading stocks because it was fun.

I still had friends going to college in Orlando, so I decided to move there and live with them. I planned to make a fresh start for myself in 2004. Orlando would be boring, but it would be the perfect place to rehabilitate myself. At the very least, the warm weather would encourage me to go outside during the trading day when there weren't any worthy plays. I realized I couldn't even remember the last time I'd gone outside in the daytime over the past few years.

From the very beginning, I enjoyed living in Orlando. I moved into a house with four college friends, and my rent dropped to about one-tenth of what it had been in New York City. The city itself was much less expensive and nobody even knew what a hedge fund was—several people told me they thought I was a landscaper! This new lifestyle removed whatever pressure I'd been feeling to deliver consistent trading profits. I planned on trading whenever the market offered up some exceptional opportunities, but no more. I'd worry about raising capital once I had stronger returns to show potential investors. This was all well and good in theory, but the market wouldn't let me off the hook so easily.

In early 2004, nanotechnology was the latest market craze, and the stocks in this sector rose substantially. One nanotechnology play, a company called Nanogen (NGEN)(*t*), had surged from a few dollars per share to the teens all within a few days. It looked like the first worthy play of the new year. One morning, the stock made a sharp downward price move and I excitedly rushed in to short. Just as I shorted, the stock price spiked higher. This was just a common morning fakeout, and I had taken the bait—hook, line and sinker. My premature entry set me up for a large loss, but I played it safe by taking it like a man and covering quickly. I continued to play this stock for a few days, but it bounced around much more than any other play I'd ever seen before.

After my first loss, I was much more disciplined—short selling only when the stock cracked any important price level to the downside—but the volatility of the sector caused multiple fakeouts, and I got caught a few times. After all, while trading rules helped swing the odds in my favor, they never worked 100% of the time. Due to the commissions I paid my broker, I ended up with an overall loss of nearly $55,000. This was definitely a case of overtrading. I had to control myself.

A few days later, when the stock price finally cracked, I was so shell-shocked that I barely had the guts to take a short position of any size, and my profits were limited.

I added to my problems by simultaneously playing several other nanotechnology companies, but that trading only resulted in further losses. Maybe New York City wasn't the problem; the problem was me. I still had not learned to control my hunger for constant profits. It was frustrating, but it was still early in the year, so there was plenty of time to make up for these mistakes. At the very least, these losses made it much easier to truly forget about fundraising and focus on Florida living.

I took some time off from trading and got back into the college lifestyle. This time around, I made sure to do it right, which was made easier by the fact that I had a boatload of cash without any classes or responsibilities whatsoever. Orlando was so cheap that I could easily throw huge parties for a few hundred dollars—so I did. My parties attained a degree of notoriety, and I was

inducted as an honorary brother into two separate fraternities. It
was as if I were back in school and in full party mode once again.
It felt great to be just a regular guy again without any business-
related worries. After a few weeks, I even stopped waking up so
early to check the markets. For the first time in a very long time,
I was free from my all-consuming desire for profits, and I enjoyed
every second of it. I worked on my golf game, lounged by the pool
and watched movies for hours on end. Even though I still had a
fund to manage, I knew I needed this time off to put everything
into perspective. I still kept an eye out for worthy trading opportunities, but none appeared.

Still concerned about generating some income, I diversi-
fied my personal assets by making a short-term loan to a private
local company whose future looked bright. The company, Cygnus Entertainment, seemed to be in position to become the next
Ticketmaster, as they had won large contracts to handle the online
ticketing for Universal Studios and AAA. It also helped that the
CFO was the father of one of my closest friends. So, I wasn't very
worried about the risk of default and I looked forward to earning
above-average interest rates on my $25,000 loan.

Overall, this laid-back lifestyle suited me. I even began
contemplating retiring from trading altogether, but I hadn't made
enough money to let go of the markets just yet. I was called back
into service when several worthy plays sprouted in the springtime.

It had been nearly two months since I had made any meaningful trades, but March and April brought several plays that were
impossible to ignore. I finally took retribution on NGEN, the
nanotechnology company that had decimated me back in January,
by successfully shorting shares when their stock cracked several

important price levels to the downside. These gains merely cut my previous losses in half, but I was impressed with my ability to delay my entry into the trade until I saw the proper price action occur—that being the afternoon fade. It was the same old story. I simply needed the patience to wait for the important price levels to crack before short selling. Over the years, my inability to follow this one straightforward rule had cost me hundreds of thousands of dollars, but now it seemed as though I might finally be able to control my impulsive tendencies.

I thought about how many plays it'd taken me to get to this point. I'd witnessed a variety of manias that had seemingly been created out of thin air—trading everything from Internet, Chinese, Japanese and security stocks to biotechnology, nanotechnology and alternative energy plays. Now, homeland security plays had become the latest craze. I hadn't played them when they rose exponentially after 9/11, because that event truly helped their businesses and I saw no potential in short selling companies that were financially sound. There's a difference between companies that actually have booming businesses and companies that just seem that way. Press releases, corporate management and people on Wall Street can exaggerate and mislead, but numbers are cold hard facts. Now I was convinced that the recent price action in this sector was based on hype and hype alone.

One such company, IPIX Corporation (IPIX)(*t*), touted their "revolutionary" security cameras by quoting a local congressman in their press releases. The congressman boldly stated he thought IPIX's cameras would better protect our country if installed on every block in America. It seemed to me that IPIX's "revolutionary" security cameras were really nothing more than

cameras with 360-degree views; I doubted they'd be very successful. But my opinion was overruled for the time being by the
market's insatiable demand for IPIX's stock. The congressman's
support helped the stock surge from less than $2 to $27 within
two weeks. The average daily trading volume swelled from a
few thousand shares to over 60 million shares during the run-
up. While I thought this surge to be a bubble just waiting to
pop, I respected the massive buying power behind it. By buying
the stock each time it broke out to another new high, I profited
alongside the momentum crowd.

When the stock price climbed from $15 to $22 in one day,
I just couldn't buy any longer; I had to short. I actually started
short selling the stock too early, at $20, but in the face of such a
ridiculous price move, I felt justified. I took a small position at
first, but as I watched my losses pile up as the stock price quickly
squeezed higher, a feeling of fear and disgust swept over me.
Within 20 minutes, the stock jumped from $22 to $27, and at
that point I had lost over $100,000. I refused to take the loss and
instead added to my position to average my cost basis higher, to
$24. Within two hours, the stock price dropped to the $21 range,
and I covered my short for a $70,000 gain.

While I was thankful for this profit, I wondered how large
my gain would've been if I had waited for the proper price action
to occur before short selling. The ideal entry point would've been
during the 20-minute period of sideways price action after the
run-up had already occurred. The sideways price action cracked
ever so slightly at $25 and it was at that moment that I should've
taken my position, because after that point there weren't any
meaningful bounces for another two days and the stock price
dropped quickly to the $16 range. I had profited once again, but

I covered too quickly because I had been so shell-shocked from being down so much money in the first place.

Many people look back at situations like these and ask themselves what if they had seen the signs earlier. My problem was that I knew exactly what to do, but in my excitement for a potentially large score, I had once again missed the ideal entry point and, worse, frightened myself into covering my short position too early. As thrilling as $70,000 in profits was, I sat in silence for nearly an hour and wondered whether I'd ever be strong enough to overcome this discipline problem.

I didn't have much time to ponder because on the very same day, another homeland security play looked ripe for the picking. Over the previous two days, Mace Security (MACE)(*t*) had jumped right alongside IPIX, with their stock price surging from $3 to over $14 on 50 million shares traded. Traders lumped these two stocks together, which was not that far-fetched considering both companies were associated with homeland security. Due to their success in the personal security market, MACE was already a household name so it was only natural for the momentum crowd to promote it as a homeland security play, too. No matter, I knew the party had to end sooner or later. I was determined to wait for the right time to short, and this time my resolve paid off.

While risking only $200,000 of my total capital per trade, I repeatedly shorted MACE so perfectly that within one afternoon, I had taken nearly $80,000 in profits. To reduce my exposure, I traded in and out of the stock several times throughout the day. For weeks afterward, I was so delighted with this trade that I wasn't very bothered by the fact that both IPIX and MACE fell by 50% over the next month. As profitable as it would've been to short these companies for the long term, I knew I didn't have the patience or the capital for that game. Finally, my rationality had prevailed over my impatience and I had made some serious profits.

In April 2004, my fund's 13% monthly return made me the industry's top performer, on a percentage basis, once again, but more importantly, in a somewhat boring market environment, my year-to-date return was nearly 10%. With money from seven investors, my fund now had $1.2 million in assets. Not bad, but I still yearned to expand my reach outside the realm of friends and family. My average position on these recent plays had been only 20,000 shares, and yet the stocks I was shorting had traded upwards of 40 million shares daily. I couldn't help but wonder what my gains would've been if I had shorted 100,000, 500,000 or even 1 million shares.

It was time to think about expanding my fund to take my trading to the next level. My 10% year-to-date return was good, but not great. I figured returns of 25 to 35% would be needed to attract new investors quickly, but experience taught me I would only lose money if I tried for too much too fast. I had profited nicely from the latest plays, but it was inevitable that a quiet period would ensue. After all, stocks were usually less volatile in the summertime and that meant I'd be tempted to trade unworthy plays. So, I committed to waiting until the fall to make any large trades; for now I'd take some time off to clear my head.

I decided to pack my bags and go on a month-long European vacation. The time off would be good for me, and if necessary, I could still trade from the many Internet cafés I was bound to come across in my travels. Besides, this would probably be my last opportunity to take a vacation for years once I redoubled my efforts to becoming a true hedge fund manager.

I'd traveled overseas many times before with friends and family, but my renewed confidence in my trading abilities helped me enjoy Europe even more this time around. Traveling with a friend, I visited over half a dozen countries before finishing my trip in Madrid. It was only supposed to be a month-long vacation, but I was having such a great time that I decided to extend the trip. I found a luxurious apartment with a private pool in downtown Madrid and rented it for the remainder of the summer. Some of my other college friends had enrolled in a nearby study-abroad program, so all the pieces were in place for a great summer.

While I still checked the markets daily, I focused my time on contacting potential investors and promising to meet them in person after returning from abroad. Without having to worry about trading, I now had time to converse through e-mail for hours on end. I was proud of the fact that I'd built my contact list up to nearly 150 people, especially since it would take only a few converts to really grow my fund. While 150 contacts after 15 months in business in any other industry wouldn't be anything to brag about, it wasn't too shabby for somebody in the highly re-stricted hedge fund world. The situation would obviously be different if I'd taken on partners or third-party marketers, but I didn't. Now, I stopped worrying about violating industry regulations whenever I contacted somebody new, and I began conversing with many more people. I subconsciously felt safer discussing my business while I was in a foreign country as if I wasn't subject to SEC rules while abroad. Its sounds crazy, but that was my mind-set.

Meanwhile, I began trading some small plays, but the lack of stability in the downtown Madrid Internet café's Internet connection forced me to take my trading profits quickly. Luckily, the markets were stuck in a deep summertime lull so there were few trading opportunities. I particularly enjoyed the time zone difference, since the U.S. markets opened in the afternoon in Spain, which allowed me to sleep late every day. I'd become accustomed to the Spanish habit of staying out past six or seven in the morning, so the timing was perfect. Their bars and clubs stayed open late, and who was I not to join in all the fun? My friends and I enjoyed these late nights out immensely, and my Spanish improved to the point where I even began seeing a beautiful Spanish girl who spoke very little English. It was difficult to understand each other, but after I consumed large quantities of alcohol, it became much easier. Our downfall came with sobriety and when she began sending me extremely long e-mails that I had trouble understanding.

By late August 2004, I'd become bored and was ready to get back to work. Cygnus, the private Orlando-based ticketing company to which I'd previously loaned money, sent me an e-mail saying they were offering friends and family a chance to invest before they went public—meaning the company would become publicly-traded.

I thought I knew the company well, so I was immediately interested. What's more, the cheap buy-in price of $1 per share made it particularly affordable. The company was still just a start-up, but their ticketing software was unlike anything I'd ever seen before. I could easily imagine thousands of companies using this software, and the fact that the company was close to profitability meant that the upside potential was huge. If they could sign a few more big-name clients, they could be wildly profitable. The company expected to go public within a few months—an eternity for me—but I was comforted by the knowledge that they'd already raised nearly $750,000 from outside investors in this round of financing alone.

The risk of Cygnus's going out of business anytime soon seemed remote, especially considering the new capital they'd raised. So, in late July I decided to put 10%, or $120,000, of my fund into Cygnus. It was risky, but I was already up that much on the year so I considered my investment sensible. My fund received 120,000 *restricted shares*, or shares acquired in a private placement that could not be sold without SEC registration or until the minimum holding period of two years had expired. My parents had also liked the company's presentation, and they invested alongside my fund.

I returned to Orlando more determined than ever to grow my fund and be taken seriously by the industry. Several industry publications wrote positive articles about me, but my wimpy little $1.2-million asset base earned me little respect. I'd begun to realize that while performance mattered, asset size was even more important. After all, it was nice to get a few people to invest a few hundred thousand dollars, but, due to size restrictions, multi-million-dollar investments in small funds simply weren't feasible, no matter the performance. While I hadn't expected to get to the top quickly, by now I would've thought I'd be able to grow my fund to the $5-million to $10-million asset range. The hedge fund industry was hotter than ever and even with the recent volatility in my performance, I still had the best multi-year track record in the industry. I needed to get to the next level quickly in order to have any shot at the big time. Action was required.

To make people understand that I wasn't just some kid who'd had success during the tech bubble, I began talking up my recent market outperformance. To increase my exposure, I wrote truthful yet non-specific articles that appeared in various industry publications. To make my operation appear more professional, I invested in a fax number and corporate domain name. I moved out of my college friends' house and into a brand-new residential development with all the latest technology. The rent and utilities were more expensive, but I was aiming high so I wasn't worried about a few thousand dollars or so in additional expenses. To show others that I had indeed been making money, I even upgraded my wardrobe and leased a brand-new BMW 745Li. This didn't change the way I traded or thought, but these superficialities appeared to be important components of the investment-wooing process.

It was around this time that several hedge funds with asset levels similar to mine were exposed as outright frauds. This was not what I needed: now potential investors would be even more skeptical of startup hedge funds. Even with my bulletproof audited returns, now it would definitely be more difficult to raise capital quickly. I was so desperate to find investors that I was literally willing to try anything. Posting great returns was the most direct action I could take on my own, so I went back to trading obsessively with the goal of building on my track record.

Throughout the summer of 2004, the markets had trended gradually higher, which now helped create several mini-bubbles in the fall. There were so many strong stocks to short that I could almost taste the profits. It was the same old story with a new twist: tiny companies rose exponentially due to the overall rising market and hype, the new twist being the way in which their stock prices were hyped.

Lately, PIPE deals had become very popular. To get the momentum crowd involved and pump up their stock prices, tiny companies issued puffy press releases. Then these companies would announce PIPE deals with institutional investors at stock prices far below their current puffed-up levels. The institutional investors would have either previously shorted shares or immediately sell what shares they could to capture the easy gains, since they bought shares at massively discounted prices. Within days or weeks of any PIPE announcement, the hype would disappear, the stock price would collapse, and the short sellers would cover their short positions for easy profits. PIPE deals had the same effect on microcap stocks as the boiler rooms of years past, even though these deals were considered legal. Once again, tiny companies, institutions and short sellers made out like bandits, leaving investors who'd naively bought into the hype with large losses.

By September 2004, I'd compiled a list of nearly three dozen potential short plays whose stock prices had all doubled or tripled even though their business fundamentals remained dismal at best. They were all probable PIPE plays. Those that weren't PIPEs were touted on the message boards as being spam plays. Either way, their puffed-up stock prices looked like they would soon collapse. When the overall market began quivering late in the month, I started a full frontal attack by taking short positions in over a dozen of these fundamentally flawed companies. But I was wrong: it was just another fakeout, and I took losses of nearly $40,000 when the market rebounded strongly. It didn't matter if my reasoning was sound; I had to restrict myself to taking fewer positions. I needed to accept the fact that it was better to short only one or two positions at a time. I stopped trading and waited. For the month of September, my fund dropped 3% on assets of $1.14 million.

In mid-October, an OTCBB-listed stun-gun maker, Law Enforcement Associates (LENF, now AID)(*t*), surged from $2 to over $6 within a few days. The company shrewdly issued press releases comparing their product with that of one of the hottest companies at the time, Taser International (TASR). It didn't even matter whether or not their stun gun worked; this was just the latest in a long string of publicity plays, and LENF's average daily trading volume surged by over 60 times, or 6 million shares. Of course, the hype could last only so long, so I bided my time and waited for the buying interest to recede. After the stock rose from $3 to $6 in two days, buyers became much more hesitant. Message board posts shifted from positive to negative and no longer mentioned their revolutionary stun gun, instead focusing on a potential patent fight with TASR, LENF's need for additional capital and the dilutive effect that fundraising would have.

I quickly shorted 30,000 shares and waited to collect my prize. I was right, but the price decline was so gradual that after three days I lost my nerve and took profits of $15,000. I didn't feel all that bad since LENF was still cheap compared with TASR, and their business fundamentals weren't as bad as the stocks I really enjoyed short selling. Besides, stem cell stocks were back in play, and they usually offered great short selling opportunities.

Stem cells may play a meaningful role in medicine one day, but the companies in this space are nowhere near having anything in the way of revenues or profits. In fact, to my knowledge, the only substantial things any of these companies have ever produced are losses. But in October 2004, the hype surrounding their breakthrough science was universal. One company, cleverly called Stemcells Inc. (STEM)(*t*), surged from $1.50 to $4.50 in less than two weeks. For many traders, it was definitely the play of the month as the average daily trading volume surged from a few hundred thousand shares to as much as 60 million shares. I played the stock nearly every day for those two weeks, scalping it for a few cents and a few thousand dollars in profits at a time by short selling and covering my positions at various prices during the run-up.

As always, I ignored all the complex technical indicators used by most traders. Instead, I bought when the stock broke out to new highs and shorted when the stock cracked important price levels to the downside. After all, simplicity was beautiful, as was my resultant $25,000 in profits. October had been an excellent month for me, but these profits barely covered my dim-witted losses from September. Thankfully, the last two months of the year would bring about the greatest price surges in microcaps since the tech bubble of 2000.

The greatest winter breakouts appeared in the tiniest NASDAQ-listed companies. Since none of these companies was worth more than $10 million to $20 million before their run-ups, it was easy for promoters and pumpers to make the case that they could be worth $50 million to $100 million. It was all based on the right press releases, price action and message board posts.

Not coincidentally, the message boards were more popular than
ever and had consolidated. Now there were only a few popular
boards with group leaders who seemed to be able to consistently
pick winners. The technology had improved, so it was much easier
to see which stocks were the most popularly debated. This had the
effect of empowering groups to be able to push the price of one
or more stocks higher, thus trapping any short sellers who got in
their way.

In early November 2004, a tiny oil company, Analytical
Surveys (ANLT)(t), was the target play of several message boards
and, specifically, three message board leaders. The stock traded
at $1 per share and had 1 million tradable shares, so it didn't
take much buying power to push the price higher. I reviewed all
the message board posts and concluded that the stock was only
hot because the momentum crowd was involved. The company
had little in the way of business fundamentals, so traders saw the
stock as a vehicle that could be manipulated higher, pushing the
price higher on daily trading volume of 6 million shares. That day,
I started short selling after the stock rose to $4 per share, which
was an incredible quadruple for the day. While I knew I should've
waited for the trading volume and momentum to die down, I figured that if I had the patience to hold for a few weeks, the stock
price would surely fall back down to the $2 range.

Unfortunately, the next day, the stock price opened near
$6 per share and I had a paper loss of nearly $100,000. Since I'd
been in this position many times before, I didn't panic and instead
added to my short. I reminded myself that this stock was only in
play because of the message boards; it had to come back down to

reality eventually. But the stock didn't listen to reason, and even as I added, the price kept surging. By the early afternoon, the stock hit $8 per share and I panicked, covering my short and taking a $220,000 loss. I just couldn't risk losing any more.

A little less than an hour later, the stock price started to downtrend. I wanted to jump back in with a large short position, but I was still too shell-shocked to trade with any size and I missed much of the stock's fall to the $6 price range. The good news was that there was now a wall of sellers at every upturn and I felt confident enough that they would remain and even increase in number, so I took an 80,000 short position overnight. Before the market close, I made back some of my losses, but I still finished the day $180,000 in the red. As bad as this was, I knew from experience that the stock price could fall much further and I could make it all back and possibly more. I'd better be right or else my fund was definitely out of business.

The very next day, due to the same message board hype, another microcap stock had surged. Monarch Services (MAHI) (*t*) was another fundamentally lacking microcap company like ANLT. Despite poor business fundamentals, their stock price spiked from $1 to $4.50 on 4 million shares traded. This time around, I waited for the wall of sellers to appear before short selling and taking a 50,000-share position overnight. The very next morning, the stock tanked nearly $1 per share, handing me $50,000 in profits.

Meanwhile, my overnight short in ANLT also acted perfectly, as the stock dropped by over $1.50 per share, and I had taken a $120,000 profit by noon. This was crazy, after being down $220,000 the day before; I had nearly made it all back and

I was down only $10,000 overall! I would've given anything to do these trades over again, but it was too late for that. I scanned the markets all afternoon for similar plays, but there were none to be found. I switched my focus back to ANLT and MAHI, since I was determined to squeeze an overall profit out of the situation. ANLT downtrended perfectly all afternoon and I shorted the stock repeatedly, earning small gains along the way. From my many trades, I managed to make a cool $45,000. MAHI was acting stronger than ANLT, and the trading volume wasn't very strong so I stayed away.

I had achieved my goal of turning an overall profit from these plays, but the swings were much wilder than I'd ever anticipated. If I planned on being successful in the future, I needed to be more disciplined. I'd learned to limit the number of my daily plays, but I needed to learn to wait until all the right variables aligned. How could I force myself to be more disciplined? I remembered the self-control I'd developed in my tennis days, so maybe I could use physical training to help me once again. The very next day, I met with a local trainer and started a daily exercise regimen—after the market close, of course.

There were other hype plays toward the end of November and beginning of December, but I wasn't about to take any large positions anytime soon. Anyway, there weren't many shares available to borrow to short these new plays, and I became worried that my short selling days might be nearing an end.

My fund was up nearly 15% on the year, and while these returns weren't great, they were solid enough to attract some interest from potential investors. After all, even though the market had had many large ups and downs over the same period, I had still always made money each year. My broker had yet to introduce me to one single investor, but I didn't blame him, considering he was privy to my wild intraday swings.

I turned to creating marketing materials to send to the somewhat steady stream of potential investors who'd begun contacting me. I now boasted nearly 200 industry contacts, but since they were mostly individuals, they were only capable of investing amounts in the hundred-thousand-dollar range.

My main target became the funds of funds, or *FoFs*, as they had recently exploded in number. These were hedge funds that invested in other hedge funds, and this diversification scheme allowed them to invest millions at a time. They brilliantly reduced the risk of portfolio loss because they consisted of multiple hedge funds that pursued various investment strategies. If there was any trouble in one of the funds in which they invested, these FoFs were well insulated from the fallout.

Several FoFs told me they liked my strategy, niche and performance, but they couldn't invest yet because of my minuscule asset size. Many of them gave me different targets ranging from the $5-million to $25-million asset range, at which point they claimed they'd be more likely to invest.

In the meantime, I worked out every other day with my trainer and hired a personal chef in the hope that the discipline required for healthy living might spill over to help my trading. Orlando was so incredibly cheap that the total cost of these indulgences was less than $1,500 per month. It would only take one successful trade to cover these expenses for an entire year. By now, my dreams of rapidly growing my hedge fund had all but faded; the business world simply didn't move as fast as the trading world. All I needed was to demonstrate a little patience and wait for further worthy plays to prove myself. I truly believed everything would eventually click if I just stuck it out.

Then, on December 26, 2004, the Asian tsunami hit.

It quickly became one of the deadliest natural disasters in modern times and had an unprecedented global impact. As was the case on 9/11, the scrapper in me subdued my emotions concerning this event and quickly began to ponder how the stock market would be affected. To watch all the video footage that was posted, I checked dozens of websites, but more importantly, I watched the message boards light up with discussion about which stocks would benefit the most from the catastrophe.

Everyone agreed that a tiny company that made earthquake absorption equipment, Taylor Devices (TAYD)(*t*), and Euro Tech Holdings (CLWT)(*t*), another tiny company that cleaned the water supply in Asia, would benefit the most. Analytical Surveys (ANLT)(*t*), the tiny oil play I had played in November, was also mentioned as a major beneficiary. When the markets opened on December 27, I cleared all the other stocks from my watch list and focused on these three plays.

ANLT's stock rose a little, but the company had recently been issued a *going-concern letter*—meaning their auditor was dubious of the company's ability to stay in business. You can imagine why this hurt the stock's potential for a large price gain. CLWT rose from $3 to $5 on trading volume of 2 million shares, but it couldn't compete with the star of the day, TAYD, the company that made earthquake absorption equipment. TAYD was rumored to be meeting with multiple Asian governments to install their equipment throughout the region, which helped their stock to surge from $2 to nearly $7 on trading volume of 12 million shares. I traded the stock all day, unsuccessfully trying to guess its ultimate top. For all my work, I ended up losing $60,000, but I knew I could make it back the next day. I didn't take any positions overnight because I didn't want to risk being caught in a short squeeze during the likely overnight gap-up.

December 28 turned out to be a great day for my little operation as TAYD predictably surged higher during the first few minutes of trading. Within a half-hour of the market open, I shorted into the mania, and a wall of sellers joined me. Many short sellers wanted to partake in these plays, so shares of this security weren't easy to borrow. Earlier in the morning, I'd wisely called my broker to reserve shares for my account. I took a rather large position of 30,000 shares at $8.25 and was quickly down over $20,000 as the stock price neared $9. But the trading volume had already begun to fade, so I added to my short position. Within 5 minutes, I was breakeven and within 20 minutes, I had taken a gain of $40,000. I tried to play it conservatively for the rest of the day, but the stock price downtrended so perfectly that I had shorted my way to another $60,000 in gains. I took several small profits by short selling the other two plays, ANLT and CLWT, bringing my daily gain to over $120,000. I loved this game!

While these profits were great, I couldn't get over the fact that I was better at making quick gains of 10¢ to 30¢ per share rather than going for more substantial gains of $1 to $2 per share. After the market close, this thinking lingered on my mind. Was I condemned to earn these small profits for life?

The good news was that my $1.3-million fund earned $60,000, or a little over 4.5%, net of fees, for December, and $230,000, or 20.36%, net of fees, for the year. Comparatively, the S&P 500's annual return was only 10.88%. I had successfully profited from the most volatile sector in the U.S. stock market, and although my trading was incredibly flawed, I was immensely proud of my work. The question remained: would this be enough to attract additional investors?

Chapter 11: The Year That Cygnus Built

The new year started out on a frustrating note. After all the excitement of the previous few months, the great trading opportunities in the microcap space evaporated completely. Whenever any play began to look interesting, I couldn't find any shares to borrow. Yes, the demand for borrowable shares had skyrocketed that quickly. As much as I craved opportunities to practice disciplined trading, there was literally nothing to do for weeks on end. I tried switching gears by buying a few breakout plays and scalping a few other plays, but overall I didn't gain or lose much.

However, my boredom was interrupted by some major news from Cygnus. The company was about to go public and had signed yet another large client: Cedar Fair, a multi-billion-dollar theme park company. Cygnus now expected to be profitable on an annual basis, as they were handling the online ticketing needs of the attraction industry's #2 and #4 players. Not too shabby for a tiny startup company. They executed a *reverse merger*—or the acquisition of a publicly-traded company by a private company—with a company listed on the *Pink Sheets*, a marketplace populated by extremely tiny and developmental companies. As a result of the merger, Cygnus split their shares 3-1, so my initial 120,000 restricted shares at $1 now became 360,000 restricted shares at 33¢.

I was now invested in a true penny stock. Experience had taught me that while price manipulation and company news could help a penny stock's price surge, any price strength was usually temporary. I ignored the circumstantial evidence, instead focusing on Cygnus's upbeat business outlook. Their blue-chip customer list made them unique because for all my pattern recognition experience, I'd never seen such a tiny company with so many billon-dollar clients. Who knew? With my luck, I might be invested in one of the few great companies to ever be listed in this marketplace.

I counted the days until Cygnus would finally begin trading, but there always seemed to be more delays. I talked with management weekly, but whether it was paperwork, legal filings, transfer agent issues or lawyer approvals, something always prevented the stock from trading. The worst part was that I didn't fully understand any of it, so I couldn't comment one way or the other. Previously, I had always been in total control of my investments so that even if I screwed up, I had only myself to blame. In this instance, I didn't have any control whatsoever, which made me very uncomfortable. My discomfort was largely an afterthought though, because SEC regulations prevented me from selling any restricted shares for another 18 months, or until July 2006.

By mid-April 2005, the waiting was finally over. Cygnus (CYGT)(*t*) debuted as a publicly-traded company on the Pink Sheets marketplace. While Pink Sheet status was typically reserved for only the tiniest and most developmental companies—particularly because they weren't required to submit financial reports with the SEC—I knew it was only a matter of time until other people recognized Cygnus's potential. While it was definitely risky, the investment represented only 10% of fund assets, so I believed it to be a risk worth taking. On their first day of trading, their stock opened at 50¢ and surged all the way up to $1.20. I had never been so excited in my life. At that closing stock price, I now had over $313,000 in paper profits.

Of course, the stock price didn't hold that price, probably because most of the initial buying was done by my friends and family who'd been influenced by my endless speeches about the company. After all, the entire trading volume on Cygnus's first day was slightly under 100,000 shares. I didn't even know how anybody could sell; only later did I discover that there were people who received boatloads of *unrestricted shares*, or freely saleable shares, in exchange for executing the reverse merger. Apparently, in reverse mergers, the awarding of unrestricted shares for services rendered was common practice, but I only cared about the current stock price, unconcerned with any extraneous details. My trading background hadn't prepared me for this investment; I greatly underestimated how frustrating it would be to have to hold my position for such a long period of time.

Cygnus's stock price closed the month in the 85¢ range, thus producing a sizable gain for my fund. I even added to my position by buying shares in the open market. I was that enamored with the company. Now they'd also announced a ticketing deal with America Online. It seemed like everybody wanted Cygnus's software. Their stock price didn't move much on this news, but I was unconcerned, since this was yet another blue-chip client who served to strengthen Cygnus's market share. In addition, even though I only had paper gains, my overall confidence grew, so I was much more disciplined in my trading. In spite of the fact that there were few trading opportunities during that month, I played them well, and the gains contributed to an 8% monthly gain on fund assets of $1.45 million.

Short selling the stocks that had risen dramatically had become extremely difficult, but I wasn't worried because I thought my newfound trading discipline and Cygnus would surely make up for any lost opportunities.

Now, I recognized how much I needed a life outside the stock market. I decided to move from my high-tech apartment into an old house nestled on a lake a few miles away. As much as I enjoyed using all my high-tech appliances, a simple Internet connection was all that was required to do my job. The new house was particularly special because the lake was connected with several other lakes, so my friends and I would be able to go boating. We built a dock out back so we could go out on the water anytime. I planned a lazy, sun-soaked summer filled with drinking, tubing and socializing. To complete my vision for the summer, I bought a ping-pong table and a grill, but I kept my trainer and personal chef to maintain the balance between relaxation and discipline.

Of course, I still kept a constant eye on the market, but I didn't expect many forthcoming plays. While the overall market was down on the year, my fund was already up nearly 13% over the same period, and these solid results helped me add another 50 potential investors to my contact list. Still, none of them seemed likely to invest anytime soon.

In addition to changing my physical location, I also made a change in my back-office operations. To administer the fund assets that weren't my own, my current fund administrator charged me 1.25% annually. This meant that if I was successful in raising additional capital for my fund, the fees would grow exponentially. While this administrator was extremely organized and had done a great job for me, I wasn't comfortable with the possibility of paying fees that could increase that much. My administrator was unwilling to part with this setup, so I parted with them instead. Since my accountant always issued his reports in a timely and organized manner and his fees were predetermined, I kept him. Now I had to find a new administrator who was affordable for a startup fund like mine.

After much research, I finally found an administrator who had an impressive client list and, more importantly, charged by the hour. They told me that my current prospectus had several errors and that they would update everything for only $4,000. As I re-read my offering documents in detail for the first time, I was surprised to see that they were indeed correct. My first administrator must've used a boilerplate document, because many of the paragraphs were out of place and there were typos galore. The overall statements were all correct, but the document definitely required some editing. How could I have been so stupid as to not notice these oversights before now? I felt ripped off, especially since I'd paid nearly $8,000 for this sloppy prospectus. I believed them when they told me to concentrate on trading and leave all the paperwork and legal filings to them. Their work had been so professional and organized that I'd taken them on their honor without ever really proofreading my fund's most important document! Could the errors in my prospectus be the reason I hadn't raised any money? There was no way to know, but the answer was probably yes. It was the latest lesson in my education as an entrepreneur: oversee every single detail of your business.

This discovery made me respect my new administrator early on, but it was only a matter of time before they also did something wrong. For a cut of any fees I would earn, they said they'd gladly introduce me to outside capital. In my two years of industry experience, whenever someone had uttered that phrase, it had killed any hope of my being able to trust them again. Still, I told them I'd be interested if they were truly willing to explore that route.

It was less than a week later when my new administrator failed to deliver the updated prospectus as promised. This time around, I'd paid only $4,000 compared with $8,000 before, but after calling them every day for nearly a week and a half, I still hadn't received the document. It made me wish I had withheld some of the payment until after the work was completed. Worse yet, when I finally received the new document, I discovered it to be full of errors, as it, too, was simply another company's boiler-plate. Was there something wrong with everybody in this busi-

ness? After going back and forth with several more rounds of ex-
cuses and drafts, we finally had a seemingly error-free document.
But I decided to stay with this administrator on the off chance
that they would raise capital for me. Besides, the cost was only a
few hundred dollars every few months. To make sure all the legal
filings and paperwork were handled properly, I brought on yet another lawyer, who came recommended by one of my trader friends.

Now, I could finally make a more professional push to find
new investors. The industry practice was to wait for investors to
come knocking, but I was tired of waiting so I decided to take the
fight to the FoFs themselves. By now, I belonged to nearly half a
dozen different hedge fund databases, so I scoured each one thoroughly in search of contacts. I wished the databases would con-
solidate, but that was just a pipe dream. Nobody wanted to share
information; everyone wanted their own little slice of the industry
pie. Since I was still a premium member of *Hedgefund.net*, I used
the information listed on their database the most. I spent a week
collecting and organizing the e-mail addresses of every FoF that
was interested in funds specializing in microcap equities, short
selling and short-term trading strategies.

I e-mailed each FoF to ask if they would like to see my
fund's details. Some replied; most didn't. I'm sure they were all
taken aback by my aggressive approach. I wasn't embarrassed; I
was determined. I knew that many people's businesses had been
built on cold-calling, and in the hedge fund industry, this was the
only way to cold-call people. For once, I wasn't worried about industry regulations, because I contacted only FoFs and they already
had many millions of dollars under management. They posted
their contact information and results on the same databases I did,

so they were fair game. I felt that if I could just get them to look at my fund, my eye-popping returns would pique their interest.

After all, I now had six years, 1999 to 2004, of fully audited consistently profitable returns. I played in a vastly underfollowed market niche and had performed well, yet I hadn't been able to raise capital from anyone who hadn't known me or my family for years. The problem was face time. At this point, I'd met with only a few dozen potential investors in person. Many startup companies in other industries meet with hundreds or even thousands of potential investors before finding any capital. And my fund definitely wasn't for everyone, so I needed to talk to as many people as possible. I had to forget about the industry regulations and go for broke to meet more potential investors.

As much as I wanted to blame my fundraising difficulties on industry norms and regulations, if I'd been honest with myself, I would've realized that my entire first year of meetings was useless—not because of any advertising restrictions, but because I hadn't learned how to properly present my fund. Before I'd discuss my fund in any detail, I used to walk into meetings with a superior look on my face and throw down a non-disclosure agreement. I was that cocky. If the roles had been reversed, I would've surely torn up any non-disclosure agreement and hoped that this wannabe fund manager would fall flat on his arrogant face.

My superiority complex had since diminished along with the risks I took and the returns I earned. The good news was that this helped dramatically improve my presentation skills and lower my risk of ruin. I was still confident, but now I was much more realistic about my goals, and I think people recognized the change and liked it. In fact, after several recent investor meetings,

I followed up with phone calls and e-mails, and some people said
they were likely to invest in the next few months. Sadly, after a
few months, nothing ever came of it. It didn't even matter; as far
as I could tell, it was all part of the game. I told myself that it
would only be a matter of time before I was rewarded, as long as
I continued posting decent numbers.

Early in the summer of 2005, I was finally proven correct when I landed my first FoF investor. For over four months,
I'd been in constant contact with this FoF, and now they finally
decided to invest $100,000 with me. It was the minimum my
fund accepted and wasn't much in dollar terms, but it was a start,
so I was content. Apparently, they found me from my premium
listing that had cost upwards of $24,000 without any results until
now. Perhaps my luck with fundraising was about to change.

As thrilling as this was, I became even more excited
in June 2005, when my old friend Internet Initiative Japan
(IIJI)(*t*) popped onto my watch list. Their stock price had
languished in the $4 range for quite some time, but it was
now back in play, surging to nearly $10 on average daily trad-
ing volume of 10 million shares. The momentum crowd had
become rather intoxicated with IIJI's proposed stock offering
in their home country of Japan. The message board consensus was that their offering would be a big hit there and raise
a great deal of capital for the company. I had no experience
with this type of news, so I was cautious. But IIJI and I went a
long way back, so I was still interested. I posted notes all over
my computer to remind myself to wait until the last possible
second before short selling.

These stupid little notes actually worked well in helping me bide my time. To make it a worthy short, IIJI needed to crack $9.50 per share, so I made that my target entry point. For nearly three days, the stock price sat just above this level in the $9.60 to $9.75 range. IIJI would tease me for hours on end, and yet their stock price always backed off just when I thought it might actually give in. During this flirtation, I had my finger on the trade trigger no less than a dozen times.

Good thing I listened to my rules because one afternoon the stock price unexpectedly surged, thus trapping short sellers and squeezing them to buy to cover their positions at higher prices. Within two days, the stock price rose to $14 on trading volume of nearly 40 million shares. I shorted into this mania and covered for gains ranging from 30¢ to 75¢ per share during the intraday price drops, but my positions, like my gains, were limited. I knew the big money would come only after the stock broke the inevitable sideways price action to the downside.

The very next afternoon, I witnessed the perfect sideways price action and waited for a break of $13 per share. The price went back and forth for nearly two hours. Before finally cracking, experience taught me it would hover around this level over the next few days. While I kept an eye on it, I didn't take it very seriously, since I didn't want to risk getting sucked into another short squeeze. Also, my trading software was equipped with a feature that beeped whenever a stock on my watch list cracked a pre-determined level. Sure enough, when I was in the bathroom less than 50 feet away, my computer started beeping like crazy. I rushed back to discover the stock price had indeed cracked $13 on its way to $12.25—all within a few seconds. I was so close to pulling the trigger to short 40,000 shares. My bathroom trip had cost me nearly $30,000!

Nevertheless, I jumped in with a small short position, but I was scared of any potential bounce because the stock price had already dropped so quickly. Later in the day, I covered my short position as the stock price broke $11, taking a small gain of a few thousand dollars. I continued to trade in and out of the stock for small gains, but I knew I'd missed my ideal entry point. Luckily, a few days later, I held a small overnight short position when the stock opened down nearly $3 per share following news that the company had cancelled their Japanese IPO due to a lack of inter-est. Now that's irony.

Instead of being early to short as usual, I was late and I lost out on the big score. That's trading for you. But I was somewhat satisfied because the gains from this play showed my new FoF investor a small monthly gain.

Meanwhile, Cygnus' stock price stabilized in the 80¢ range. By now, I'd almost forgotten about it, since the trading volume had dried up and there were still 13 months to go before I could sell the vast majority of my position. In late June 2005, I was reminded of my position when the stock price jumped to the $1.20 range on record trading volume of over 600,000 shares. I immediately took a small gain on the shares that I had bought in the open market because there didn't seem to be any news to account for this rise. Just when I didn't think it could get any better, Cygnus announced they'd won a contract to handle the online ticketing for Hershey Park, yet another major theme park, and the stock price rose to the $1.40 range. I bought a few thousand more shares in the open market because I knew this to be a huge win for the company.

Just a few days later, message board posters began detailing the flood of Cygnus spam they'd received regarding the Hershey Park news. It sounded as if someone was pumping this play. My experience with spam plays had only been from the short side, but I knew that stock prices often tanked after the spamming had come and gone. I prayed this wouldn't happen to Cygnus. Over the next few days and weeks, I was delighted to see the Cygnus's stock price hold its gains. This price strength made me even more of a believer in the company.

My fund's gain for June 2005 was slightly greater than 15%, or $270,000, on assets of over $2 million. Once again, not only was my fund, on a percentage basis, the industry's top monthly performer, but my 30% gain on the year now placed me in the top 1% of all funds. Also, two new investors—a FoF and a wealthy individual—jumped aboard with $100,000 each, so my fund finished the month of June with over $2.2 million in assets.

Everything was going extremely well, but I was determined not to let up. Getting my fund over the $2-million asset mark opened some doors, but I still couldn't get any large investors until I reached the $10-million to $20-million asset range. After posting my latest results, I quickly scheduled several investor meetings in New York, Georgia, Texas and California. I needed to close some new investors soon because my traveling expenses were really adding up. Unfortunately, most of my meetings were in New York City, which was the most expensive city of all. While the meetings went well on the whole, due to my minuscule asset base, nobody seemed seriously interested in investing with me anytime soon.

Apparently, size really did matter—at least in the hedge fund industry. While everybody liked my returns and niche, they wanted to put a minimum of $1 million to $5 million to work, and due to the industry regulations, my fund couldn't handle investments of that size. After all, this particular regulation prohibited FoFs from owning more than 25% of any one fund's total assets, effectively crushing my chances at any quick asset growth. I was in a catch-22 situation. I couldn't raise money because my fund wasn't large enough, but my fund would never grow large enough if I couldn't raise money.

The only way to grow my fund without any large institutional investors would be to receive investments from wealthy individuals. However, industry regulations made that a time-consuming process that could take years to accomplish. No wonder the third-party marketers were so cocky about their pay-to-play business model.

Maybe I should borrow money or combine my fund with another fund in order to grow our total firm assets. I desperately began exploring all the possibilities, but my research led me to believe that any kind of borrowing or merger was too risky.

Feeling dejected by this turn of events, I returned to Orlando without any new investors and with nothing to show for my trips but several thousand dollars in expenses. While the bills paled in comparison to my current income, I hated to spend money with nothing to show for it. I was getting an education in how the startup hedge fund world really worked, and it wasn't pretty.

In mid-July 2005, a worthy trading opportunity distracted me from my worries. A tiny company, Host America (CAFE)(*t*), issued a press release claiming that Wal-Mart was testing their energy-saving lightbulbs in several locations for potential expansion into a significant number of Wal-Mart stores. This news sounded incredible, and many traders became rather excited. I, on the other hand, was not impressed. Over the years, I'd seen hundreds of puffy press releases and this was a shining example. But for the time being, the bulls won, with CAFE's stock price surging from $3 to over $9 on average daily trading volume of 20 million shares—all within four days.

I began short selling the stock in the $9 price range. There hadn't been any sideways price action yet, but the trading volume had faded and experience taught me that stocks tended to reverse direction after they tripled in value within one week. In addition, the large price increase opened the door to the possibility that the SEC would step in and halt the stock to ask for more information from the company. I'd seen many trading halts over the years, and they almost uniformly resulted in the stocks in question tumbling by more than 60% when they finally reopened—if they reopened at all.

Unfortunately, this stock still had some momentum, so when the price broke out to a new high at $10.50, many short sellers, including me, were forced to cover. We trampled each other to try to cover our short positions and get out, but like most short squeezes, our desperation added to the momentum buying, pushing the stock price higher to $16 on average daily trading volume of 30 million shares. I escaped in the $13 price range, but I had still lost more than $120,000 on the many short positions I had taken at various points during the run-up. Apparently, I was fated to have to endure these mammoth losses before I tried to make them all back.

As always, I knew I'd have another chance to short this play, so I bided my time and waited. Surprisingly, the stock managed to hold near its highs, so I restrained myself and waited for a break in the sideways price action before short selling. Just a few days later, I was incredibly angry when the SEC halted the stock at $14, asking for more information from the company. The stock didn't reopen for another two months, and when it did, the price was $5 per share—a perfect short selling opportunity wasted. The SEC made the company publicly disclose that they hadn't signed any contract whatsoever and had only a verbal agreement! It was laughable: a press release and a $125-million market valuation all based on a verbal agreement. Meanwhile, several company insiders bailed out at inflated prices, so several lawsuits were initiated. My fund is part of one of the group actions; the case is still pending.

Luckily, I had gained from trading several other, lesser plays in July thus softening the blow to the fund from the CAFE hit. In addition, Cygnus continued moving higher, albeit slightly, so my monthly loss amounted to little more than 2%. Two more FoFs jumped aboard to invest $100,000 each, and fund assets, even with the monthly loss, climbed to $2.5 million.

In the previous month, Cygnus had signed deals with no fewer than five major attractions, so their future looked brighter than ever. I'd dreamed about this little company dominating the ticketing industry by either becoming the next Ticketmaster or being acquired by them. Now it seemed like a real possibility. The attractions industry appeared to realize that Cygnus's ticketing software really was superior to the other options out there.

Even Ticketmaster had never signed so many attractions in such little time.

At my fund's current asset levels, I believed my trading could always provide a few hundred thousand dollars annually, but Cygnus could make millions for me. I allowed myself to think big, since I now expected a large price increase in Cygnus's stock over the next year, especially if they moved to a larger exchange.

Since I was so confident about my upcoming gains from the Cygnus investment, I figured I'd need to take full advantage of my impending profits and use them to raise as much outside capital as possible. And the best place to do that was the hedge fund capital of the world: New York City. While I didn't want to leave the good life in Florida, I knew I had to be where the big money was if I really was going to grow my tiny fund. I was more mature and comfortable now to handle both the energy level of New York City and the undeniable presence of hedge fund politics, so I believed I was ready to take another shot at the big time.

Chapter 12: I Love New York!

From the very beginning, my move back to New York City
was a complete mess. The city's vacancy rates were at an all-time
low, so when I finally found a suitable midtown apartment, I
jumped on it. Fortunately, I was first in line at the broker's office,
ahead of nine other people who applied within a few hours' time.
Nonetheless, four days before I was supposed to move in, I still
didn't have a signed lease. My broker calmly explained that he was
in daily contact with the landlord and we'd sign the lease in person the day before I moved in. I thought this incredibly strange,
but I believed my broker because he said this was how New York
City real estate worked. While the moving trucks were already

on their way, my broker changed his tune and informed me that the landlord no longer wanted to rent the apartment because he was more interested in selling the entire building. After cursing my broker out and threatening legal action, I stormed out and scrambled to find a new place.

I was lucky enough to find a $4,500-a-month penthouse just a few blocks away. In fact, the new place was a much better deal than the old one. The only problem was that the new apartment needed to be refurbished and wouldn't be ready for another month. I spent the day I was supposed to move into my new apartment, working to divert the moving trucks to my parents' house in Connecticut. I succeeded and temporarily moved back in with my parents. For the time being, my dream of being at the epicenter of the hedge fund world would have to wait.

September 2005 was slow in terms of trading, but I received the fantastic news that one of the FoFs with whom I'd met a few months back wanted to invest $500,000 in my fund. This was my biggest score yet and would push fund assets past the $3-million mark. Maybe the money spent traveling and premium *Hedgefund.net* listing weren't wasted after all. The FoF's one condition was that they wanted one of the major auditing firms to be my fund's auditor. Sure, no problem. Even though the new firm would do the exact same work as my current auditor while costing me $15,000 more per year, I understood this was all about trust and perception. I needed a big-time auditor to attract large investors anyway, so I met with several potential auditors and prepared to spend more money.

To my utter delight, the FoF's wire transfer appeared on time in my fund's bank account. The very day the wire hit, Cygnus's stock hit an all-time high at $1.58. My mother cooked a great meal, and my family and I sat around discussing the future. This was a time for celebration. My $3-million fund, through September, was up over 30%, net of fees, on the year. The future never looked brighter.

The day before finally moving back into New York City, I flew back to Orlando for a meeting with Cygnus's management to make sure my optimism was still warranted. While industry regulations prevented them from discussing any specifics, they said they were in negotiations with several more companies that would further solidify their market share. I wanted to impress my new investors with gains, so my fund made a short-term loan to Cygnus for $250,000 because it seemed to be an easy way to accumulate added interest without much risk. I figured that earned interest, which I'd previously looked down upon, was a great way to earn some extra cash during quiet times.

For the first time, Cygnus had publicly posted their financials, and they actually seemed pretty solid. Quarterly revenues were only $1 million, but the company's quarterly losses were less than $100,000 so the risk of them going out of business anytime soon seemed remote, especially considering their recent customer wins.

Trading opportunities remained scarce, with few worthy plays and even fewer borrowable shares. When taking a short position, the lack of borrowable shares now forced me to perfect my timing, since I wouldn't get a second chance. The market had now matured to expose my worst fault as a trader. I used to average my cost basis higher whenever I entered a position too early, but now that was no longer possible. While I tried to adapt to these new rules, I suffered only small losses in the process.

Even on the rare occasion when I shorted at the perfect price, the gains barely covered my losses from the trades that I had timed incorrectly. While I was worried about this marketplace change, I figured I would surely find a new way to profit, just like I had always done in the past

By October 2005, I'd moved into my midtown Manhattan apartment and was ready to take on the city and make further industry contacts. In case a potentially worthy trade appeared, I didn't want to network during the trading day. So, I limited my meetings to the nighttime by going out every night, with a newfound maturity, and striking up conversations with anybody who worked in finance. I quickly found that talking up my fund to potential investors and industry insiders was a waste of time. I always followed up with the people I met, but most of them could barely remember our conversations, or if they did, they seemed unimpressed with my fund's tiny asset base. While nearly everybody was still polite enough to ask to see my marketing materials, I received the same response time and again: contact them again only after I reached the $5-, $10- or $20-million asset range.

Since trading was slow and I'd gone through my cable provider's list of movies on-demand, I allowed myself to network during the trading day. I attended conferences, luncheons and any other Wall Street gatherings I could find. Individual tickets to hedge fund industry conferences were in the $1,500 range—far too rich for my blood—so I was forced to attend free functions hosted by various brokerage firms and service providers. Understandably, these firms would only help raise capital in exchange for commissions. I'd gladly give my business to them, but they didn't have any borrowable shares to short. That was a dead end.

The good news was that within a few weeks of living in the city, I'd made a great many connections. I became acquainted with hundreds of small-time brokers, lawyers, traders and other hedge fund managers because we were all in the same boat: trying to grow our businesses.

One time, I was invited to a regular hedge fund manager meeting where managers presented their top investment ideas. I didn't fit in because I never knew when my plays would appear, so I recommended money market funds, the safest investments around. They didn't like that. It didn't matter because while talking shop with these people was fun, they were more concerned with raising money for themselves anyway.

I attended capital introduction parties thrown by one of my brokers, but these events turned into hedge fund managers pouncing on the few FoF managers and wealthy investors in attendance. The investors and FoFs left quickly, and we were left to drown our sorrows in the open bar.

Next, I tried to contact the people I'd met when I first started my fund, but nearly every one of them had gone out of business or changed firms. Those who were still in the industry thought it odd—considering my continued market outperformance—that I hadn't been able to raise any assets. I told them how I also thought it was odd, so many of them agreed to ask around on my behalf. I followed up with them repeatedly but never heard back from anybody.

Through sheer determination, I gradually befriended several industry big-timers, but after I told them about my strategy's inability to handle more than $100 million in assets, their enthusiasm dwindled. It was amazing that everybody considered my goal of eventually expanding to the $100-million asset range too limiting to be worth their time. I couldn't understand it; to me this was big money.

I was tired of putting so much time and effort into cultivating relationships that got me nowhere. I needed to think big and spread my message to thousands of people at a time; ideally, those interested in what I had to say would take the initiative and contact me for once. So, I started to develop relationships with journalists in order to get my story out to people who might actually want to invest with me. While I'd previously attracted the attention of the mainstream media through my *CBS Marketwatch* article, now I wanted to catch the eyes and ears of the new segment of the press that focused specifically on hedge funds, wealthy individuals and traders.

The magazine *Trader Monthly*, started by a former trader, was a kind of financial *GQ* geared toward those who were able to make great amounts of money in the finance world. I read through this magazine as eagerly as I'd pored over the pages of *Beckett Baseball Card Monthly* so many years earlier. *Trader Monthly*'s annual "Top 30 under 30" list, in which the magazine profiled the top 30 people in finance under the age of 30, came out that fall, and I was shocked to see many people I knew make the 2005 list. In fact, I was somewhat outraged because some of their funds were even tinier than mine. I immediately contacted the article's reporter to set up a meeting with her to make her aware of these facts. She agreed to meet me.

When we met, she told me she was impressed by my passion and my story, so she promised to recommend me for the next year's list. I was ecstatic; my ego might actually be right for once, as I probably deserved to be on this list. I felt bad for not having pursued any publicity earlier, because this was just one example of places I could exploit in my quest to find potential investors. And I desperately needed investors.

After all my gains—a 67% return since fund inception—I had only earned approximately $100,000 in fees over three years. Subtract startup costs and fund expenses and I might've been up $40,000 or so. So much for my dream job! If I couldn't expand my fund soon, I might as well just manage my personal capital and axe this costly hedge fund structure. Over the next few months, my mission was now to meet many more journalists as I had no intention of missing out on easy publicity again.

By the end of the year, my broker finally came through with an introduction to a potential investor. Unfortunately, he was based in Florida, so I needed to fly back down for the meeting. I didn't mind too much because it gave me the opportunity to see my many friends who still lived there. I spent several days in Orlando catching up with everyone and then drove down to Miami to meet my broker and this potential investor of his.

I was skeptical until we pulled up to the community in which this investor lived. It was incredible. I allowed myself to feel just a glimmer of hope. As I shook hands with an overly tan older fellow who had bleached white hair and large diamond-studded earrings, visions of receiving a $500,000 or $1-million investment raced through my head. He was a classic Miamian. Surely he'd give me a chance to make some money for him.

We had a productive lunch as I explained how I shorted microcaps, and most importantly, we talked about Cygnus's bright future. He was clearly most interested in that topic. By the end of our meeting, I felt rather confident that he might actually invest in my fund.

I returned to New York City, excited by the possibility of additional capital, but over the next few weeks, my potential investor and I had several conversations, in which he always told me he needed a little more time to think things over. Days turned into weeks, and weeks turned into months without any investment whatsoever. After a few months, I never heard from him again.

Meanwhile, Cygnus announced a major ticketing deal with Expedia, but the stock price didn't budge. I forwarded this incredible news to dozens of traders and journalists, but nobody seemed to care; Cygnus was just a tiny Pink Sheet–listed company. I didn't need them anyway; I knew this one deal would be worth tens, if not hundreds, of millions of dollars for Cygnus. After all, Expedia's primary business was airfare and hotel booking, not attraction booking. Cygnus specialized in attraction ticketing so it was a perfect match. A partnership between the two companies would open up an entire new market segment to Expedia and, in turn, help make Cygnus's print-at-home ticketing become the industry standard.

It was just so beautiful that I wanted to invest personally now, too. I pulled $90,000 from one of my two safety CDs, even though I had to forgo some interest as a penalty for my early withdrawal. I personally bought 100,000 shares of restricted stock at 90¢ per share, since Cygnus's future now looked even brighter. I wouldn't be able to sell these restricted shares until late 2007, but since the shares were restricted, I received a nice discount to the current market price of $1.50. My father strenuously objected, but it was difficult for him to argue with me, since I'd been right about this company thus far.

But within a few weeks, in late December 2005, I grew worried when Cygnus's stock price declined to the $1 range. How could people be selling? Cygnus now had deals with Expedia, AOL, Universal Studios, Cedar Fair, Hershey and AAA and was teetering on the edge of profitability. How many more deals with blue-chip companies would it take for Cygnus to finally get some respect?

Of course, the problem wasn't that there were so many sellers; there just weren't many buyers. The fact that Cygnus wasn't listed on a major exchange was definitely a problem. I cannot deny that I felt a kind of kinship with Cygnus because we were both successful, but people still doubted us because our operations were so tiny. Of course, my operation had now been profitable for seven consecutive years, while Cygnus's had yet to make a dime, but they could easily overtake me once their deals ramped.

I tried to step back and analyze the situation without bias; the biggest problem I saw was Cygnus's lack of exposure. They'd announced deals with AOL and Expedia, but neither press release had included the ticker symbol of these Internet powerhouses. I tried applying my publicity play rules to the situation, and that made Cygnus's stock seem even more undervalued. A price spike was inevitable if Cygnus's press releases could just get a few momentum traders interested in their stock. Soon, Cygnus would be selling millions of tickets through Expedia, and the subsequent press releases and revenue figures would surely create a sensation. It was only a matter of time.

Following this reasoning, I stepped in and added to my fund's position at these lower stock prices. The fall in Cygnus's stock price was entirely to blame for the fund's 6% loss in December, but my $2.75-million fund still returned 23.56%, net of fees, for 2005. Comparatively, the S&P 500 index gained 15.79%. My fund's return was slightly better than all the other major indexes, too, but my trading gains amounted to only $52,000, my worst year ever. Aside from my gains in Cygnus—some of which were realized but most of which were still on paper—I had drastically underperformed the overall market. I had yet to find a way to overcome the difficult trading environment for short selling and relied on the gains from Cygnus. I truly believed this one investment would propel me to the next level in 2006.

Chapter 13: Pink to Red Ink

My fund's short-term loan to Cygnus was scheduled to
be paid back on December 31, 2005 and the CEO had said he
was confident they'd be able to repay the loan on time. In the
days leading up to the loan repayment, I repeatedly called my
contacts at Cygnus, but nobody answered. I tried to comfort
myself by visiting the websites of the company's major clients to
make sure Cygnus was still handling their online ticketing. To
my surprise, Universal Studios—Cygnus's largest customer—
had now redesigned their website and appeared to be handling
their online ticketing themselves. I broke into a cold sweat. This
didn't look good.

Now I frantically began calling Cygnus every few hours, and after three tries, I finally got the CEO on the phone. He calmly informed me that the funding they were working on hadn't come through as expected but that it would most definitely be in place if I could just give them one more month. While they'd lost Universal as a client, everything was still chugging along because their recent deals would make up the difference. He pointed to a recent press release that confirmed that Harrah's, the casino giant, was now testing Cygnus's software to handle the entertainment ticketing in their casinos. He also said the Expedia website should be ready shortly, which would obviously be a major boon to the company. While I was nervous about this situation, I didn't want to convert this loan into stock because I would've received a huge number of restricted shares that I'd then have to wait two years to sell. I did the only rational thing I could: I enforced a penalty that required them to owe my fund additional interest and gave them one more month to come up with the money.

My overwhelming optimism for this investment now diminished. To better understand Cygnus's troubles, I devoted the first few weeks of 2006 to researching the ticketing industry in detail. While it appeared Cygnus had several competitors, the competition possessed incredibly inferior software. The main risk was that the attractions might choose to save money by handling ticketing themselves. This was the apparent route that Universal had taken. But no matter how much I researched, I couldn't predict whether companies would choose inferior ticketing technology just to save money. To lower my risk, I continued to sell my unrestricted shares all throughout January.

By the end of that month, I wished I'd sold more aggressively because Cygnus's CEO now informed me that the company still couldn't come up with the money they owed my fund. Concerned I'd never get to see a dime of my loaned out capital again, I converted the loan into a boatload of shares at discount prices, receiving a mix of both restricted and unrestricted shares. I had no idea whether the company would be around long enough for me to sell the restricted shares in two years, but at least I'd be able to begin selling the unrestricted portion immediately to get what money I could out of this situation.

Even though the safest course of action would be to sell all my shares as quickly as possible, I was still somewhat enamored with the possibility that new clients like Expedia would help Cygnus turn profitable and make my investment worthwhile. Clearly, this was a game in which my lack of experience hurt me. I'd been mistaken to apply my trading rules to this private-equity-type investment.

By the end of February 2006, the stock price dropped to 75¢. The situation went from bad to worse when the CEO called to say Cygnus was running out of money and needed $75,000 to make it to the summer. By then, the commissions from their ticket sales and the Expedia deal should deliver enough cash flow to allow them to remain in business. Due to the scalability of their business model, the upside was enormous. Other company insiders promised to match my $75,000, so the total money raised should definitely be enough to enable Cygnus to make it to the busy season.

I concluded that Cygnus had a solid chance at staying in business and turning profitable so I invested $75,000 more in exchange for more restricted stock. Unfortunately, the other company insiders never came through with their side of the deal, so Cygnus was still short of funds! The CEO and CFO allegedly now tapped into their own savings and invested the remaining $75,000, but there was really no way for me to confirm whether they did or didn't. All I knew was that the company stopped calling me for money, so I assumed they somehow raised enough cash to survive for the time being. I tried to increase my rate of selling but, due to the illiquidity of the stock, I could unload only a few thousand shares daily.

While all of this was going on, *BusinessWeek* contacted me to say that they wanted to feature me in an upcoming article. The magazine planned to feature several hedge fund managers to show the myriad of Wall Street outsiders who'd started their own funds. I excitedly agreed, and for nearly two hours I talked with the magazine's reporter about my financial journey. By the end of our conversation, I still didn't know exactly what, if anything, she would use. I tried to stay calm, but I knew that this one article could help turn everything around for me. The exposure should help me find investors, and any increase in capital would subsequently reduce my fund's exposure to my investment in Cygnus.

Of course, my lawyer didn't like any of this, since the article might be construed as advertising, which industry regulations strictly forbid. He said the press was free to write anything about my fund, but according to industry regulations, I wasn't allowed to comment. That's why everybody in the finance industry said, "No comment!" While I was tired of keeping quiet, I still wasn't quite ready to publicly thumb my nose at industry regulations. I made it clear to the reporter that to avoid the possibility of legal action, she shouldn't use any performance data. While the rules were unclear as to what exactly could or couldn't be used, a public display of performance seemed like a potential offense.

When the issue hit newsstands in early March 2006, *BusinessWeek* had ingeniously included some of my returns as an exhibit from one of the hedge fund databases in which I posted my returns. The article inspired dozens of younger investors and wannabe managers to contact me, but I shooed them away because my focus was on potential investors. Stupid kids, didn't they know I had a business to run? Unfortunately, the article had a slightly negative tone about the lack of transparency in the startup hedge fund world and didn't generate any investor interest.

In late March, I wasn't very surprised when Cygnus's CEO called to say the company needed one more $100,000 investment to make it to the summer. He claimed to be in negotiations with another blue-chip company that would finally push Cygnus into profitability. I agonized over whether I should give up and accept the 30% loss for my fund, in addition to a great personal loss, if the company were to go under. This was a classic case of a startup company's running out of money before their deals ramped. Because Cygnus lacked the funds they needed to finish the audit, they were unable to attract any outside investors. The vast majority of startups in such a situation had gone under; who was I to think this time would be different? No matter how I sliced it, this wasn't a decision to be taken lightly.

After much deliberation, I decided to invest an additional $100,000, bringing the Cygnus position to approximately one-third of total fund assets. I was obviously troubled by the increased position, but it was a calculated risk: investing another 3% of my fund's capital to avoid a potential 30% wipeout. My fund received a mix of restricted and unrestricted stock by assuming control of shares owned by a company director that were now freely tradable. I didn't require a board seat as part of the deal because I still wanted to be able to sell my shares as quickly as possible.

It was an educated gamble, but that's basically what I'd been doing ever since I started trading anyway. The difference here was that my experience was in trading, not venture capital or private equity. Two years ago, I never would've imagined that my short-biased fund's largest position would be a Pink Sheet–listed security that could seemingly go out of business at any time, yet here I was, adding to this position and praying that this latest round of financing would stem the company's bleeding once and for all. I checked my fund's prospectus to make sure this investment conformed to my fund's policies, and thankfully it did.

As I continued to sell what Cygnus shares I could, I adjusted to this new reality. I lowered my cut of fund profits from 30 to 20% in a futile attempt to attract new investors. I cut every extra expense out of my life, including my New York City lifestyle. It wasn't paying off anyway. For weeks on end, I basically didn't leave my apartment except to go running in Central Park to make myself feel physically healthy, even though I was miserable.

As much as I wanted to blame Cygnus's management, I could really blame only myself. Cygnus was like many other Pink Sheet-listed companies: simply trying to survive. As a responsible hedge fund manager, I was the one who should've known better than to invest so heavily in such an operation. The falling stock price prompted several heated discussions with my friends and family, since they had also invested. I tried to make them understand that I was in much more trouble than they were, but this elicited very little empathy. The investment was going south, and they couldn't stand to lose their money. If I'd been in their shoes, I probably would've been just as upset. If Cygnus went under, the 33% hit to my fund wouldn't be a total disaster, but I'd definitely be out of business.

Fortunately, in early May 2006, Six Flags (SIX), one of the world's largest theme park operators, announced they'd be selling tickets on AOL's ticketing website, AOLTickets.com, through a partnership with Cygnus. I was cautiously optimistic, as I'd heard this kind of good news before. My concerns seemed justified when Cygnus' stock price failed to react to this incredible news. At the very least, I now estimated that Cygnus would survive through the summertime.

Later in the month, my hopes surged once again, with the announcement that Cygnus had been selected to handle the online ticketing for all 28 Six Flags theme parks on SixFlags.com. This was hugely important—the deal ensured Cygnus' survival—but again, Cygnus' stock price failed to react. As in the past, the press release hadn't included the Six Flags stock ticker, SIX, so nobody really cared about the news. If Cygnus had been a NAS-DAQ-listed company, momentum traders would be all over this press release, and the stock would've become a worthy publicity play to short into after the stock price had risen enough.

Adding to the problem, the Expedia deal never went live as promised. Although Cygnus' management never offered any official explanation, I heard dozens of different stories from various industry professionals who speculated as to why the deal had fallen through. I never learned the truth, but it didn't even matter anymore. At this point, all I could do was reduce my exposure by selling shares, even though the stock price had fallen to the 40¢ range by June and the 30¢ range by July. My fund's position was now under 25% of total assets, and through the end of July, my $1.85 million-fund was down 9% on the year. Unfortunately, this entire debacle had greatly damaged my reputation within the industry and compromised my ability to take on any more risk.

By midsummer, the three-year-old bull market had strengthened, so there were several potentially worthy short plays. I figured I could help my situation, albeit slightly, by trading profitably that would further reduce Cygnus as a percent of my fund's total assets. Unfortunately, finding borrowable shares was more difficult than ever because there were only 5,000 to 10,000 shares available of my target stocks on any given day. This suited the risk-averse stance I'd adopted, but my timing would have to be impeccable. Luckily, my broker began offering *preborrows*, or the ability to reserve shares for future short selling, so, for a small cost, I could re-short these shares as much as I liked, on an intraday basis. This new ability greatly increased my profit potential, but I didn't really utilize it because I was too afraid to take on any large positions.

Around this time, I fired my fund administrator because they'd completely stopped responding to my e-mails and phone calls. I became suspicious when I received notices of payments due from several states in which my fund was supposed to be registered. The SEC didn't require managers with under $25 million in assets to register nationally, but I was supposed to be registered with agents for legal process in all the individual states in which I had investors. When I called the agencies of the states in question, I discovered my fund was registered but that my fund hadn't always paid on time. I was incensed. I'd always sent checks to my administrator to send to the states on my behalf for this exact reason. These annual fees ranged from only $10 to $200 but were extremely important in a business sense. So, I severed relations with my administrator and asked for all my records. I never received a response.

Luckily, my administrator shared an office with my broker, so he helped retrieve my files. I went back to my first fund administrator because I knew that that firm would at least keep all my paperwork and legal filings in order. As a perk for coming back, the firm gave me a password-protected website free of charge. The firm's fee structure for taking a percentage of assets managed hadn't changed, but I doubted I'd be raising any large amounts of capital anytime soon.

After nearly a year of courting the press, my efforts finally paid off when I was named to *Trader Monthly*'s "Top 30 under 30" list for 2006. Since the previous year, the magazine had grown substantially, so this list was accorded much more credence this time around. The buzz from my magazine contacts was that I was on the short list to be the cover boy when the issue finally came out. I did a photo shoot for the magazine, but I didn't want to get my cover hopes up because there were also nearly a dozen other traders at the shoot. I would just have to wait and see when the new issue debuted a few weeks later.

In the meantime, I told *Trader Monthly* I'd be willing to do whatever they needed to help promote the issue. Most traders on the list worked for other people, so they couldn't give quotes to journalists seeking comment. This opened the door for me to run my big mouth. So, when *Reuters* and *Institutional Investor* ran stories about the list, I was the only trader quoted. Even though there wasn't supposed to be any order to the list, my quotes helped give off the impression that I was number one. For once, the restrictive industry regulations helped me!

When the issue finally hit newsstands, I discovered I wasn't the cover boy. I wasn't even close to being the most successful person on the list. In fact, I probably deserved to be at the bottom of the list. For their respective funds, most of the other traders managed hundreds of millions or even billions of dollars. The list, like the hedge fund industry, had definitely come a long way in one year's time. Still, the magazine had liked my scrappy story and my personality enough to believe that I could successfully promote the issue, so they arranged to have me and another trader appear on CNBC. CNBC! After all, appearing on that channel had been a dream of mine since I was a teenager, because CNBC was to financial professionals what MTV was to musicians.

Here I was, a startup hedge fund manager finally getting the chance to tell my story to the world three years too late. Oh, how I wished I'd been in this exact same spot when my confidence allowed me to bet large and daily profits were commonplace. But now the timing was all off. Still, I had to take what life had thrown at me. My lawyer and I agreed that I shouldn't mention Cygnus at all, even though it would definitely help the stock price. Nonetheless, this was still going to be a once-in-a-lifetime opportunity, and I knew I would enjoy every second of it.

I was so nervous before going on that I needed to have a few drinks to stop shaking. Even though I wasn't filming from the main studio in New Jersey, the satellite feed meant my interview would be beamed into 95 million households in the U.S. and Canada in real time.

My segment was nearly five minutes long, but it went by in a flash. It reminded me very much of the time I'd gone skydiving, because the adrenaline overtook me and my brain couldn't immediately process my surroundings. After it was over, dozens of friends and family members were quick to congratulate me on my relaxed screen presence. I chuckled to myself as I thought about how I owed my laidback attitude to a few shots of vodka. The other featured trader on the segment wasn't as fortunate, and his awkwardness made me look even better.

I was actually quite lucky with this turn of events, but it was just the beginning of my publicity spree. All afternoon long, I fielded e-mails and calls from dozens of people interested in my fund, but when we got down to it, they were mostly just young people who wanted advice or to work for me in some other capacity. This time around, I talked to everyone because I really had nothing better to do. All of this newfound attention was gratifying, but since industry regulations kept my details secret, outsiders didn't realize how insignificant my little fund was. They knew only that I was a young hedge fund manager getting a lot of press. They had no way of knowing that I still worked in a bathrobe from my apartment, my strategies worked better when I was more comfortable taking large risks, my target niche wasn't very scalable, my one major investment nearly failed and nobody was interested in placing any substantial capital with me anytime soon.

Days afterwards, I'd grown tired of the phone calls and e-mails from young investors wanting career advice and help with their trading. I really only wanted to talk to potential investors. Several interested parties contacted me, but the majority never certified that they were accredited, so I wasn't able to tell them anything about my fund. It was ridiculous; all my hard work to get publicity had finally succeeded in finding people interested in my fund, but due to industry regulations, I couldn't tell them anything. While I knew I couldn't accept them into my fund, these non-accredited investors probably had wealthy relatives and friends they could steer my way. My lawyer said he was proud of me for not giving in to the temptation of discussing my fund, but I felt only disgust and disappointment. My CNBC debut was a great moment in my life, but it didn't help me in a business sense. Accomplishing one of my childhood dreams turned out to be more bittersweet than I could have ever imagined.

Chapter 14: I am a Warrior

The best part of all this recent media coverage was that it introduced me to two producers who'd been contracted to produce six episodes of a show called *Wall Street Warriors* (WSW) on the high-definition television channel MOJO. It would be a reality show that explored the lives of people in finance who worked hard and played hard, and they thought I might be a good character for a few scenes. MOJO wasn't a very well-known network, because people needed a high-definition television set to watch the channel, and such sets were still too expensive for most people. Nonetheless, they still had 6 million subscribers nationwide, so the show would surely be seen by a few people.

The producers planned for me to appear in one episode, but after filming me for a day, they said they wanted to film me several more times. My lawyer advised me not to appear, but by this point I was so fed up with the industry ban on publicity that I couldn't have cared less about ruffling feathers at the SEC. In a half-hearted attempt to placate the regulatory powers that be, I made the producers promise not to use my fund's name or any of its financial details, but that would be my only conciliatory action. The opportunity to star in a TV show was just too exciting to pass up.

Smack in the middle of my Cygnus-induced depression, we filmed nearly a dozen times over the latter part of the summer. The cameras followed me everywhere, including filming memorable scenes of my getting up in the morning, trading from my living room, pitching a potential investor, kicking over a fan after losing a large investor, going out on a date, throwing a rooftop party, enjoying a lavish dinner with my friends, having my mom clean my apartment and golfing with my best friend. The experience was particularly enjoyable because it allowed me to blow off steam and it was therapeutic for me because it put everything into perspective. For all my problems, I was still in pretty good financial shape. And maybe the show would catch on and I would become a reality TV star. Crazier things had happened before.

Wealth was preferable, but nothing wields power in New York City like celebrity status. The chances of it happening were slim, but I was determined to ham it up as much as possible to give the producers some interesting footage. I didn't mind making a fool of myself on national TV; it would only help my case if the SEC came down on me by claiming that I was advertising my fund to the general public. By the time I finished filming, no sane person would ever be able to call my performance a business advertisement.

The editing process lasted a few months, so the show didn't air until late fall 2006. The producers, whose previous credits included a documentary about a famous porn star, barely understood the world of finance, so I looked forward to seeing their take on our industry.

When the episodes finally aired, my trading sequences didn't really make a whole lot of sense, but overall I think they did an excellent job of portraying my life and those of the other characters. We all seemed to be obsessed with money, which was very accurate, at least in my case. The show's other featured personalities were much more careful about allowing the cameras into their personal lives. After all, they weren't being filmed in the middle of a personal financial crisis. This had the inadvertent effect of propelling me to become the star of the show.

The New York Observer, a small but influential local newspaper with a circulation of 50,000 of New York City's movers and shakers, managed to get a pre-release clip of the show and contacted me. Their reporter wanted to meet me in person for a quote or two. It wasn't one of my brightest ideas to sit down for an interview on a Sunday morning after a late night out, but I managed to become the star of the story—probably as a result of my half-drunken interview. Even though I came off as a cocky, self-absorbed finance-type, I also came off genuinely dedicated to the business, so I hoped that this might attract a few investors to my fund. The paper also gave the show a positive review. I learned long ago that there's no such thing as bad press; as long as people watched the show, there was a chance that I could benefit from it.

This article strengthened the daily stream of young investors and traders who contacted me. This time I talked with everybody because I wanted to help teach them about the realities of the industry. Tulane even recognized my newfound fame and began sending students my way whenever they requested contact with alumni with hedge fund connections. Again, I was again bombarded with calls and emails from young people who thought I was their "in" to the hedge fund industry. Some of these students were naive enough to think that they could invest as little as $500 in a hedge fund. They really had no idea how trading and hedge funds worked—I felt like Kinsey educating people about sex. I obligingly answered everybody's general questions about the industry at large, no matter how absurd.

I think I shocked the majority of my fans by advocating extreme patience, understanding and conservatism. The Cygnus debacle had made me infinitely more cautious and I hoped to save others from making similar mistakes. Not to mention that the last thing I needed right now was for some teenager to lose their life savings by trying to duplicate my trading results. That kind of excessive risk taking was not for everybody, and that was something I needed to make sure people truly understood. A few months earlier, my financial future had been falling apart, so I couldn't have cared less about helping other people. Now that Cygnus had survived and I'd accepted the hand I'd been dealt, I wanted to help others because it felt good to give helpful advice. I knew from experience that nobody else would talk to these young investors without having some kind of angle, such as wanting to

sell expensive seminars, programs or investments to them. On
the other hand, I wanted to talk about my experiences earnestly
to educate these kids. For the first time in a very long time, my
life had meaning.

Outside of my life as a financial celebrity, I spent my days
looking for the best prices at which to sell my Cygnus shares.
Even though I still had many hundreds of thousands of shares, I
knew I had to get rid of them all to avoid further losses.
In early fall 2006, Cygnus had finally reported a $200,000 quar-
terly profit for the first time, but this positive news still didn't
attract any buyers, and their stock price continued to slide lower.
Selling my shares was a long, drawn-out process, but I didn't
really have much of a choice. The situation had already hurt my
returns enough to make several investors withdraw from my
fund. Fund assets dropped below $1.5 million, and by mid-fall,
my fund was down nearly 15% on the year.

My reality show had begun airing weekly in October 2006,
but over the next several months, it was re-broadcast several
times daily. I ended up starring in five of the six episodes, so I
estimate my episodes have already aired in excess of 700 times.
The one upshot about being featured in a television show on a
little-known network was that it continually thrust me into the
spotlight time and time again. The network even crafted entire
promos around me, which only helped to increase my exposure.

I met my fans everywhere: at the gym, in line at the phar-
macy and at restaurants, random people would come up to me
and shake my hand. In order to pick my brain, they bought me
drinks and took me out to fancy dinners. Every guy wanted to

hear all my stories and get an introduction to the "hot" female lead of the show because not only was she beautiful, she was also rumored to be an industry power player. Others wanted me to pose with them for pictures. This type of hero worship reminded me of my freshman year at Tufts during the tech bubble, but instead of profits, my fans were now interested in entertainment. Instead of fielding questions about which stocks to buy, I was being asked about how specific plotlines from the show panned out. It was all kind of stupid and surreal, but it definitely was fun.

Now that I was a pseudo-celebrity, blogs began debating whether the incredible returns of my past would continue. They had no idea about Cygnus. My fund suffered several down months in a row, so it became the prevailing opinion that my celebrity status had affected my trading. Even *Trader Monthly* ran a negative article about me, noting my fund's recent losses. What none of these publications or bloggers knew was that the pieces were in place for my downfall long before they even knew my name. Cygnus had sucked whatever ability I had to take on risk so that trading hardly even impacted my overall returns anymore. Opportunities came and went, but I felt comfortable taking only small positions—quickly locking in any profits when they reached a few thousand dollars and thankful that the additional capital lowered my fund's exposure to Cygnus.

But no matter how many skeptics came out of the woodwork, the phone calls and e-mails kept streaming in from people who'd been inspired by my story. I became more determined than ever to tell them the whole truth so they could see all the potential risks and rewards. I advised them to start reading as much as possible so they'd be better prepared for when opportunities arose, as they inevitably would. These teenagers still believed in me and in their own optimism about their futures. I hoped that my story would help them understand that trading and hedge funds were tricky businesses but that with enough patience and hard work, the rewards could be great.

As I explained the industry to more and more people, I began to regain confidence in my trading abilities. After all, trading was in my blood and I couldn't let it go completely. Even though I'd lost my appetite for risk, worthy trading opportunities came and went as my strategies still held true.

In early November 2006, a tiny Chinese company, E Future Information Technology (EFUT)(*t*), had IPOed in the U.S. markets, pricing their stock at $6 per share. On opening day, the stock price popped and settled into a steady groove in the $12 range. The message boards began buzzing about the company's solid business fundamentals and minuscule market value, enough to interest many buyers. Within four days, the stock price climbed all the way to the $45 range. This incredible move was made possible by average daily trading volume of nearly 10 million shares. It was definitely the stock of the moment, and I played it back and forth thousands of times. I was caught in a somewhat difficult position, because the stock's indicators all pointed to further upside, but short selling was still my expertise.

I decided to trade the stock from a bullish stance, and after several months of not having any large gains, I was suddenly experiencing daily swings of $10,000 and $15,000. These moves paled in comparison to overall fund assets, but after a few days, I was frustrated because I couldn't hold onto my gains for very

long. I couldn't believe it. I had made $5,000 or more on nearly
a dozen trades, yet I had just as many down days, negating any
profits I had made. After several days of going back and forth
with nothing but thousands of dollars in commissions to show for
it all, I stopped trading and decided to wait until the stock price
cracked $30 per share. That was the key level the stock needed to
crack to the downside to be a worthy short play. Unfortunately,
the stock price decided to hang around the $35 range for the rest
of the year, so, for the time being, there was nothing for me to do.
It took nearly three months for EFUT to crack $30 per share, but
when it did, the stock price slid all the way down to the $15 range
within a few weeks. Despite this price slide, I barely touched it.

Later in the month, another seemingly worthy play emerged
in a small tool company, Consulier Engineering (CSLR)(t), whose
stock price jumped from $4 to over $10 within one day. While
the stock usually traded only a few hundred shares daily, it traded
nearly 3 million shares during this price surge without any news.
It was clearly some type of pump, whether it was message board
hype, boiler rooms or e-mail and fax spam, I didn't know and I
didn't care. By now, I'd seen so many of these kinds of plays that I
knew a crash was inevitable, so I wanted to short the stock before it happened. I started short selling gradually at first because
I didn't want to risk much capital, but in the last hour of trading,
I stubbornly added to my short position as the stock price surged
higher. I was focused on this stock's daily percent gain, which at
$14 per share was nearing 300%. It was just too much; there was
no way it could hold. Or so I believed.

What little risk management skills I possessed finally
kicked in when I became frighteningly aware that I had a $50,000

paper loss. So much for not taking large risks. As much as I wanted to hold, I knew I didn't have the guts to risk any further losses.
Within minutes, I had taken my losses, only to watch the stock
price fall gradually over the next hour to close nearly $4 lower, at
$10.44. Within a week, it pained me to see the stock trading in
the $5 range. How could I have been so stupid? To make a great
deal of money, all I needed was patience and courage, neither of
which I currently possessed.

I continued to look for trading opportunities, occasionally
taking small positions, but the game had changed for me. Opportunities came and went, but I couldn't risk losing any more capital. By restricting myself to taking only small positions, I wasn't
making much money, but I wasn't losing much either. For the
time being, my once up-and-coming fund was in serious limbo.

By November 2006, Cygnus had finally turned the corner
to consistent profitability, announcing profits of nearly $300,000
for their third quarter. This was their second consecutive quarterly profit, but nobody cared because the figures were still small
and their stock price had gotten crushed over the previous few
months. While I knew there were a few other sellers present, my
selling was definitely the main reason for the large price drop.
The stock price was in the 30¢ range in September, 25¢ range in
October, 20¢ range in November and now the 15¢ range by year's
end. By the end of 2006, Cygnus represented less than one-eighth
of fund assets, as I'd disposed of over 500,000 shares.

My falling returns scared away many of my fund's investors, including all of the FoFs. For the year, my fund finished
down nearly 26% on assets of $1.2 million, and the future didn't
look very bright. Granted, it was only one down year, but it would

be another year or two before I'd be able to sell the rest of my Cygnus shares and get back to generating any substantial trading profits. I thought about closing my fund and simply trading my personal account, but it cost me only $20,000 per year to stay in business and there was still a chance at redemption. Against all odds, Cygnus was still alive and kicking and the potential upside was still huge. Besides, the money market interest and management fees upon which I once looked down covered nearly all of my fund's expenses.

In the meantime, an increasing number of opportunities for publicity began to present themselves. *Dealbreaker.com*, an Internet-based Wall Street tabloid, was repeatedly featuring me, resulting in dozens of articles within a few months' time. Options University, a company that taught options trading, wanted me to be the pseudo-celebrity speaker at their upcoming investor conference. The Online Trading Academy, a company that taught all kinds of trading, wanted to meet me to talk about possible synergies. My show's producers even called to say that our show had been picked up in France, Germany and South America and they were negotiating three more international deals, which only meant more publicity. A few days later, MOJO announced the show was popular enough to be worthy of a DVD release in late April 2007. Nice. Not to be outdone, VH1, the television network dedicated to music videos, now e-mailed me to say they loved my story and thought I would be perfect for their upcoming *The Fabulous Life* episode that would feature the lives of the richest financial professionals on Wall Street. Wow! I had made a few million dollars over the past few years, but in no way did I deserve to be on a show celebrating the richest people in finance. Still, I didn't say no.

The steady stream of publicity opportunities reminded me of the tech bubble, when there were plentiful trading opportunities. The trading opportunities still existed, but I couldn't take advantage of them. Instead of playing the trading game, I was now playing the publicity game. I was the youngest—and basically the only—hedge fund manager willing to talk to the press, even if my fund was incredibly tiny. I would take advantage of any opportunities I could get.

Not everything was easy though. After going back and forth for weeks, the VH1 producers stopped replying to my e-mails. It's likely that they checked around and discovered how tiny a fund I managed. Oh well—one opportunity down, many to go. Just like EISQ of years past.

It was around this time that I started to write this book. I had been thinking about writing for some time, but having grown tired of the public's misconception about financial speculation and hedge funds, I now had the motivation to write an entire book. This would be my opportunity to set the record straight. For nearly a decade, trading had been the focal point of my life, but now I found it more fulfilling to educate others. I began to realize that fund management and obsessive trading weren't as satisfying as they had once been for me—I wanted to inspire and teach people.

Within a few days, I was surprised to find myself thoroughly enjoying every second of the writing process. It was great to finally be able to detail my business without worrying about industry regulations. And, every time I wrote a page, it brought me closer to my goal of finishing. I relished the fact that once I had finished telling my story, I would finally be responsible for something tangible that would be one of the only books to honestly educate people about all the potential risks and rewards of trading. As I tried to put my life into perspective, I began realizing that the lessons from my experiences, if told honestly, could help millions of traders, investors and industry outsiders better understand financial speculation. I couldn't imagine anyone else would risk their future with such brutal honesty—I would be the only one.

This book became the reason to get up in the morning. I enjoyed working toward accomplishing a concrete goal for a change. In telling my story, the learned numbness—a result of my financial roller coaster ride—gradually evaporated, and I felt as if I were truly living once again. Besides, applying my trading skills to the publishing world, I saw an incredible number of opportunities—after all, trader or writer, I will always be a scrapper.

The industry regulations that had prevented me from detailing my business had hindered everyone else in my profession from sharing theirs as well. Sure, there had been a few books about financial speculation and hedge funds, but they all dealt with great success, failures and amounts of money. Their educational value was compromised by industry regulations, their authors' day jobs and their inability to detail specific investments. On top of all that, nobody ever detailed the experiences of funds with under $100 million in assets. And yet it was those funds that comprised the vast majority of the industry and that had suffered the most from industry regulations. Most importantly, the lessons in those other books weren't very applicable to the millions of amateur investors and traders who played the market with more modest amounts of capital. My book would speak directly to this otherwise neglected demographic.

Looking back, I saw I'd foolishly gotten into the hedge fund industry thinking I could easily grow my operation to the $20-million to $50-million asset range based on performance alone. I would've saved a great deal of time, energy and money if somebody had written a book like this to educate me as to the realities of the financial world I was entering. My book could potentially save millions of newcomers from their own greed and ambition. Finally, I had a purpose again: it wasn't to become the industry's top trader or hedge fund manager but to help others learn from my experiences and pull the curtain back on this greatly misunderstood profession.

As I finished the first draft of my book, my fund was already down nearly 8% on the year through February 2007. Due to my inability to risk any further damage to my fund's remaining assets, I hadn't traded much in the new year. My continued selling of Cygnus shares had brought the stock price down to the 10¢ range. The good news was that they'd just announced a partnership with NCR Corp. (NCR), a $10-billion company. Just the latest in a long string of blue-chip partners; hopefully, this one would work out. The press release seemed promising and I was glad that somebody from NCR was quoted—that meant the alliance was real! Not surprisingly, Cygnus' stock price failed to react to the news.

Meanwhile, my publicity continued to inspire thousands of young investors and traders to contact me, wanting to learn about trading and hedge funds. Thanks to my disenchantment with industry regulations, I was really the only person to whom these youngsters could turn for any honest information. I made sure to use my newfound influence for good. It would be my ultimate act of charity and my chance for vengeance against the industry regulations that so deliberately clamped down on the spread of information. I was determined to get the truth out and nobody could stop me.

In early March 2007, CNBC called, asking me to appear as a guest commentator for their "Million-Dollar Portfolio Challenge," an online stock-picking contest that had attracted 375,000 contestants vying for a $1-million grand prize. Apparently, one of the producers had seen a clip of my brief CNBC appearance from the year before and was impressed with my performance. She wanted me to pick some plays for a half-hour segment, and if I did well, I would become one of the weekly guest commentators for this contest for the next three months. I instantly accepted. I knew this audience included many of the people who I believed could benefit most from my experiences.

I could barely contain my excitement when the CNBC Town Car arrived at my apartment to bring me to their studios in northern New Jersey. It was an hour-long drive, so I spent the time practicing everything I would say, and the time seemed to fly by. This was my one chance to make my entire hedge fund experience worthwhile. My story could help all the wannabe hedge fund managers, traders, investors and other people who, as industry outsiders, weren't given an opportunity to fully understand trading or the hedge fund industry. The industry was so tight lipped that my experiences would probably even enlighten many industry insiders about the intricacies of the startup hedge fund world.

When the cameras began rolling, I didn't even flinch. I was paired next to an important financial advisor and a best-selling financial author, but their enthusiasm couldn't match mine because I was on a mission. I spouted out all of my picks with confidence and clarity while also mixing in a little humor. The network executives said I did a great job, so they asked me to return. Perfect. I had secured a weekly spot on the most influential financial network in the world, with a probable audience of 375,000 people. I quickly went to work designing my personal website, **timothysykes.com**, mostly to share my library of over 300 finance books—and, of course, for publicity's sake.

My website went live two days before my second weekly CNBC appearance. Directly on the main page, I stated my new mission in life: to share my trading and industry experiences to help inspire and educate others. After my previous week's CNBC appearance, I had been buried in e-mails, so I knew the momentum was building. In the hope that they would write articles about me, I sent links to my website to several major financial blogs.

Dealbreaker.com came through in their usual comedic style with a feature article, and within a few hours, my website's traffic had surged to over 6,000 hits. That day 350 people signed up to my e-mail list— ironically, the exact number of contacts it'd taken me nearly four years to achieve during my time in the hedge fund industry. People were hungry for information and I was going to give it to them.

As a result of all of this exposure, a major publisher had already offered me an advance of $35,000 for my story, but my control over the finished product would be negligible and more importantly, publication would be at least a year away. That was an eternity!

No—I couldn't stand by and do nothing as the public's mistaken beliefs about financial speculation and hedge funds continued. My financial journey had taught me more about people, greed and life than I ever thought possible—I owed this misunderstood profession everything. I would repay my debt to trading by becoming its greatest advocate. No longer would people be prohibited from learning this business just because they weren't wealthy. No longer would the SEC be able to stereotype an entire industry as risky and inherently dangerous. No longer would inaccurate stories appear in the press without hedge fund managers being allowed to refute blatant fabrications.

This is what I came to realize:

We brave souls who engaged in the fine art of financial speculation were always better as a result. Win or lose, everybody benefited in some way whether or not we realized it at the time. Even though I had made many mistakes, I valued my financial journey in its entirety because my gains made me wealthier while my losses made me wiser. Hedge fund managers should not be forced to live in fear of industry regulations any longer. We should be free to discuss our businesses with whoever shows interest—and without the fear of penalty or censorship.

Getting this message out to the general public is too important to wait any longer! I simply could not wait an entire year, so I decided mainstream publishing was not for me.

Instead, I read up on the self-publishing industry and thought I had found another incredible opportunity. If I went this route, I would have total control over my book as well as quadruple profit margins, and I could get my message out within a few months. And I could do it all myself, just like I had always preferred. So I created my own publishing company, BullShip Press, LLC. The name was inspired by all the BullShip around me: the BullShip hedge fund regulations, the BullShip that influenced stock prices and the BullShip state of education in the world of finance.

My future in the hedge fund industry no longer mattered. Even though hundreds of thousands, if not millions, of financial professionals shared my distaste for the industry's regulations, I would be the only one speaking about it publicly. While I would have plenty of supporters, they wouldn't dare risk their careers and step into the firestorm I was about to create. In the name of the freedoms on which our nation was founded, I would sacrifice my future in the only profession I had ever known. I probably would've been a hedge fund manager for the next 50 years and, in time, learned enough discipline to make another fortune. But those earnings would come at a cost: the cost of freedom of speech. It wouldn't be worth it. Industry regulations needed to change, and I needed to do my part to make that happen.

As I thought about all of this during one of my regular rides to the CNBC studios, my cell phone beeped. I received an e-mail from *Wallstrip.com*, an Internet-based show that mixed finance with humor. They wanted to do an interview with me. I said I would get back to them. Cool—yet another opportunity for publicity. It seemed that my path was now set. I was on my way to becoming a public figure.

As I walked into the CNBC studios, I basked in the glow of my increasing celebrity. Nobody knew it yet, but I was preparing to fight the good fight, and it felt great. Nothing could stop me now. In the dressing room, I wasn't very surprised to see several famous financial figures getting ready for the show. Everybody had a unique story about how they had gotten there. This was the big time and even if I had reached it in an unconventional way, I was part of it now.

As I entered the *green room*, or room reserved for the guests of the show, I noticed a familiar person lounging on a nearby couch. I immediately remembered him: he was the trading coach I had met at the multi-billion-dollar hedge fund's headquarters at the beginning of my hedge fund journey nearly four years earlier. By now, I had incorporated many of his theories into my trading, saving me tens of thousands of dollars. And I was about to appear alongside him on live national TV. He advised billionaires—and my fund had never crossed the $5-million mark. This was just too much! I quickly reintroduced myself and told him the story of how we had met so many years before. It seemed like a lifetime ago.

He vaguely remembered me, and while walking to the set, we talked about our shared passion for historical business books. The cameras were about to start rolling, but I quickly asked him if he would read my book and offer a review. He obligingly agreed and we exchanged business cards. The set lights turned on and the cameras began rolling. I smiled as I knew my message would be heard.

Chapter 15: Lessons Learned

My net worth is approximately two-thirds of what it was when I was at the top of my game. It's been a long time since those wild days. I was young, naïve and proud—the worst combination for a trader. I treated trading like a video game—constantly trying to set the high score. I wanted to conquer each level in record time. Ironically, my parents' wishes have finally come true, as trading *has* taught me the value of a dollar, which, for better or worse, means that I've abandoned my video game mentality. Reality has set in. As such, my hedge fund days are over too, but I'm still in the finance game—and that's what counts.

For the time being, my financial situation prevents me from taking on very much risk in my trading. However, a time will come when I will be in a better position to take full advantage of all the worthy opportunities out there. Only then will I pounce. Thankfully, my mistakes were not made in vain, as they have taught me to be more patient and less headstrong. Despite my previous misconceptions, trading is not about who makes the most money in the shortest amount of time; the real winners are the people with the steepest learning curves, who can quickly apply their knowledge to the opportunities before them. Don't get me wrong, my losses haven't been easy to swallow. However, each hit I've taken was a necessary stepping stone in my quest for success. As such, I have now amassed a considerable amount of capital and a great number of lessons to bring to my next endeavor, whatever and whenever it might be. The future is uncertain and I have no doubt my education is not complete.

Financial speculation has the potential to create immense personal wealth, and the success I've enjoyed is not magic. I believe anyone willing to put in enough time to do the research required to learn the intricacies of the marketplace can make a ton of money. However, that is not to say that any specific strategy will work every time. It's all about dedication, timing and, most importantly, balance. The lessons I've learned over the past nine years are, to a certain extent, oxymoronic, but they represent the tightrope act that every successful trader must learn to perform. For example, while I cannot over-emphasize the value of learning from those with experience, experience sometimes becomes obsolete in today's constantly changing environment. So, you need to learn from the past, while at the same time be cautious not to live in it. Sometimes, in order to beat out your competition, you will be forced to blaze your own trail, shunning experience to follow your gut. However, there is one thing that I now know every trader must develop in order to determine when this unconventional path is warranted: discipline.

Allow me to repeat myself—the most important quality for a trader to develop is discipline. As you've read, my stubborn ego and impatience prevented me from achieving lasting success and financial security. I hope my story has shown you that any fool can get lucky and quickly make a great deal of money. But, if playing the stock market was always that easy, there would be no need for research and hard work. Considering that all the information you need to be able to profit is available on the internet, what sets successful traders apart is their ability to wade through all the muck. With regard to your sources, keep an open mind. As my losses demonstrate, if you allow your emotions and ego to control your trading, you are doomed to fail.

My greatest losses have always resulted from trades motivated by anger, revenge and pride. After a bad trade, rather than calling a time-out and giving myself an opportunity to regroup, I chose passion over reason and forged ahead, trying to will opportunities into existence, even when a more rational part of me knew I had lower chances of success. In these moments, my ego made me forget to respect the market and I was seriously injured in my attempt to control it. In this way, the interaction between you and the market is very much like a romantic relationship.

The worst time to look for a new partner is when you're on the rebound. Your judgment is skewed by feelings of anger, loss and rejection, which inevitably results in poor decision-making. In retrospect, anyone who has been part of a failed relationship can tell you that at these difficult times, the wisest decision is to take some time off to reflect on what went wrong. Similarly, your failed "relationship" with a particular trade can teach you many lessons about yourself and the market. But, as is the case with any relationship, you cannot wallow in self-reflection forever. Once the dust has settled and you've studied the errors you've made, find your center and get back out there.

While my lack of self-control turned out to be my own worst enemy, it's my hope that my story will inspire someone smarter and more disciplined to create a fortune from nothing. And, as with all of my dreams, I believe this can be accomplished. After all, my trading strategies are still viable. Penny stocks that interest the momentum crowd will continue to enjoy extraordinary peaks and valleys. As long as there are gullible people out there, there will be tiny companies attempting to boost their visibility through whatever means possible and professionals gunning to exploit their efforts. Whether you prefer buying or short selling, this marketplace offers plenty of volatility that can be used to your advantage. Of course, there are many pitfalls to watch out for. Be warned—professionals earn their living by preying on amateurs. Do not stray from your discipline and remember to monitor liquidity—if you need an example of what happens when you ignore these two rules, flip back and reread every paragraph where I've written the word "Cygnus."

This is why I urge you, please learn from my mistakes. Scrutinize them; internalize every detail until you almost feel as though they are your own. I cannot over-emphasize the importance of learning from the missteps and oversights of those who came before you. I think people are too embarrassed and fixated on reputation to admit their errors to the public. But, by brushing over their shortcomings, authors in every field do themselves and their readers a disservice. Writing this book has put everything into perspective and even taught me a thing or two. Since I've learned from my mistakes, why make someone else learn these lessons the hard way? How will the industry, or the world for that matter, advance if people are unwilling to share what they know? Remember, learning is difficult; but without it, losing is easy. This is the reason why I am so unabashedly honest about all my experiences, good and bad. I truly believe that as a reader, you will derive the most benefit from hearing about the blunders I've committed throughout my financial journey. While I might be one of the only "experts" in my field to detail my greatest mistakes, that does not change the fact that everyone makes them—and you will too. Hopefully, I can at least save you from a few.

While market study is important, it can lure you into a false sense of security; if there's one constant in the stock market, it's that everything can change on a dime. Opportunities come and go so do not overstay your welcome in any one play or strategy. The greatest opportunities stand out above the rest. With that in mind, do not get so wrapped up in your research that you try to create something that isn't there. Before many traders even take a position, they guarantee their inevitable failure by allowing their obsessive research to cloud their objectivity. After putting in countless hours, days and sometimes even months of hard work, these traders aren't open to the possibility that they may be wrong in their assumptions. They're unwilling to admit that the most effective course of action might be contrary to their thinking. Trillions of dollars have been lost by people who refuse to adapt to the marketplace. A trade can always turn around in a hurry, but only fools bank on their ability to predict these turnarounds. I warn you, short-term trades that turn into long-term holds inevitably become sources of great anguish. Sometimes you need to accept defeat and move on to new plays. But, even when there aren't any new opportunities to move on to, it's still better to sit on the sidelines and wait for the next one to come along.

Let's be honest—older people believe that the younger generation needs to exercise caution and pay their dues in order to be successful in this business. Certainly, many young startups and Wall Street whiz kids have defied such logic, but for the most part, people take this advice and get started in finance much too late in life. If I had a family to support when I first started trading, I never would've been able to take the great risks or withstood the significant losses that proved to be the benchmarks of my career. Investors and traders are born, not made. Sure, we need to learn from the mistakes of others, do thorough research, avoid half-baked ideas and understand that the odds of great success are against us. But even if we fail, we succeed because we learn important lessons early and remember them for the rest of our lives. Therefore, a case can be made that it's actually prudent for young people to take on great risk—the exception being those who cannot afford to risk any losses whatsoever. My story seems to inspire young people to want to get started in finance. Good. I hope this is the first of many entertaining books designed to help young people achieve their financial goals.

I never would have guessed my lifelong goal of becoming a fund manager would be the first step, not the last step, in the journey of my life. But I've gotten this far by keeping an open mind to learning and taking advantage of the opportunities placed before me. If not for my extreme stubbornness, I would've applied many of the lessons in the books I read to help me work through my discipline problems. In my case, books have helped, but they still could not save me from myself. I will consider this book successful if it helps just one person from making similar mistakes. I discovered long ago that the best way to compete with businesspeople who have decades of experience was to read through every business book I could find. The money saved from their lessons makes it time well spent. Just like researching investments, we should also research investment professionals. Instead of making a financial investment, the only requirement is the investment of time. Firsthand experiences are obviously preferable, but when unavailable, learn from the experiences of others. I've posted my entire financial library on **timothysykes.com.** Go there and learn from the businesspeople who've taken the time to tell you their stories.

I hope this story also inspires other hedge fund managers to detail their experiences. Learning is only possible when investment professionals step forward to share their knowledge. Hedge funds are not as scary as everyone believes—there just isn't any detailed information out there. There's too much money in this industry for investors not to fully understand the specific strategies used. Fund management is not the great mystery our legal disclaimers make it out to be. But take a lesson from me; while it's relatively easy to start a hedge fund, it's even easier to fail. You cannot go it alone, for it takes a team to build a truly lasting company. The hedge fund industry remains unfriendly to startups and does not appear likely to change anytime soon. No matter what's right, rules and regulations are not easily changed.

"Past performance is not indicative of future returns." This standard disclaimer—which appears far too often—is a ridiculous statement. What other measure of success is there but a well-documented, current track record? Let's compare this to baseball. Not surprisingly, this sport—which has been posing in place of finance as our national sport—does not use disclaimers. Can you imagine a sports commentator, saying "He's hitting .350 this year, but then again, batting average is not indicative of future hits"? Of course not; that would be ridiculous! If a major-league player has a lifetime batting average of .325 for more than five years, it's logical to assume he'll bat over .300 one more year. Barring any crop of incredible new pitchers or major injuries, the odds are in his favor. Likewise, we need to apply reason to finance. Barring any major market shifts, strategy changes or personal tragedies, it's logical to assume that a trader who's earned 20% annual returns for more than five years will earn at least 15% one more year. The future is uncertain, but a better disclaimer might be "Past performance *is* indicative of future returns." Doesn't that sound better?

As in sports, I think the general public should be allowed to see each hedge fund manager's exact stats. I'm not just talking about SEC filings, monthly and annual percent return and assets under management, but all of the details, actual dollar figures, earned and unearned income, percent of capital risked, leverage used and all the rest. Think about how many minute details are available about sport figures. Since finance is our true national sport, investment professionals should have the equivalent of our own trading cards and jerseys. A sort of National Hedge Fund League. Maybe I'm going a little overboard, but you get the point. Financial speculation, in all its forms, is what drives our country. Instead of advocating secrecy, we should do everything possible to encourage widespread participation.

In the hedge fund industry—under the guise of protecting gullible investors from excessive risk—regulations discourage participation. Since when did investing not involve risk, especially as far as the stock market is concerned? Life itself is risky. Investors should be free to choose their own investments based on solid research and freely available information. For instance, if you're comfortable with the volatility and upside potential of short selling and recognize the downside risk, you should seek out financial professionals who have a demonstrated ability in this strategy and let them manage whatever portion of your capital you'd like to devote to this strategy.

Short selling in particular is deemed a risky endeavor because of the potential for loss that is greater than the initial investment. I've researched every investment all the way back to the beginning of time, and I feel confident in saying that no investment has ever gone to infinity. Again, it depends on the skill of the trader, whose track record will speak for itself. What's a hedge fund manager who specializes in short selling to do? Wait patiently, slowly making contacts over the years as regulations change and worthy opportunities pass him by? No, hedge fund managers should be able to raise capital freely to take full advantage of all the opportunities that are available!

The irony of it all is that mutual funds may actually be riskier than hedge funds and yet they are free to advertise and talk to the press. According to their charters, most mutual funds aren't allowed to short sell or engage in other investment strategies that are perceived to be speculative, so they're allowed to advertise their "safe" products to everyone. Their television commercials emphasize their wisdom, experience and rock-solid investment expertise. But all that insight still didn't protect them just a few years back, when the markets tanked and they were unable to hedge their bullish bets. Within a few years time, thousands of mutual funds lost over half their value. The hedge fund industry has never experienced such widespread losses. Hmmm, might an inability to hedge your bets be considered risky? Mutual funds have an obligation to be bullish in their investments, and as a result, their downside risk in changing market environments, especially bearish ones, is substantial. Hedge fund can trade freely so our only concern is industry regulations.

The restrictions concerning the availability of hedge fund information apply to the otherwise freewheeling Internet as well. In order to prevent non-accredited investors from peeking in and being seduced into investing "beyond their means," regulations require hedge fund websites to be password protected. Imagine what would happen if the U.S. Food and Drug Administration restricted expensive restaurants from posting their menus online unless their diners were at a certain income level and sent forms requesting access? In addition, bona fide restaurant reviewers would be unable to share their evaluations of restaurants because their reviews would be restricted to only the wealthiest of diners. It wouldn't matter if a potential diner was simply curious or wanted to look at the menu on behalf of a wealthy friend or relative. Sounds absurd, doesn't it? But that's how industry regulations limit access to hedge funds.

Our industry has earned such special privileges because we deal directly with money and leverage, so we require special limitations to protect unworthy investors from their own greed. In late 2006, in a move that is supposedly designed to protect investors, the SEC voted to raise the asset accreditation minimum for hedge fund investors from $1 million to $2.5 million. The rule exempts venture capital funds and other startup businesses. This new hurdle conflicts with the less-than-stellar stats of the general investment business community concerning safety of investment. Take startup companies: 9 out of 10 fail in their first year, 7 out of 10 restaurants fail within the first six months and 7 out of 10 movies lose money. I don't even need to quote any sources because it's common knowledge. Investors frequently lose their entire investments, yet these industries now have lower investor minimums and are free to disclose their business plans to a wide audience of potential investors without the same kind of restrictions that hamper hedge funds. Often, their self-promotions include wildly exaggerated projections that are based less on performance than on hype and promises of huge returns for their investors. And I won't even get into the ability of escorts and alleged miracle-drug companies to advertise freely. It's appropriate for the SEC to police our industry for exaggeration and fraud, but they should reward freedom of finance for the overwhelming majority of funds that comply with the law.

Add up all the estimates of hedge funds that have opened and closed, and you'll find that less than 1% of hedge funds have ever blown up, or lost everything for their investors. Again, the data can only be estimated—ironically, due to the lack of available information—but give or take a few percent, these statistics fly smack in the face of the media's allegations that hedge funds are the riskiest investment vehicles around. The truth is that many funds close due to poor performance or their inability to raise sufficient capital. But in nearly every case, they still return their investors' money—usually with only small losses and sometimes even gains. Due to industry regulations and the media's craving for big stories, the public hears only about the catastrophic failures and frauds or the great successes of the largest hedge funds—never about any of the industry's smaller players. What's worse is that hedge fund managers aren't permitted to comment on stories, thereby invalidating nearly everything written about this industry. If I were an industry outsider, these kinds of headlines would certainly scare me. Even though a few people seem to be making great amounts of money, I'd be too afraid to invest in hedge funds. After all, the stories portray funds using incredibly risky strategies that don't outperform the overall market and could very well lose everything. On top of this, the industry seems rife with hucksters and scam artists. Stories about the majority of hardworking managers just don't sell newspapers and magazines. Is it any wonder that after reading all these skewed headlines, the general public is so fearful of hedge funds?

Fortunately, large institutions don't give much credence to this kind of misinformation. As investors who manage billions of dollars, they're more interested in returns on their massive investments. Unlike the archaic mutual funds, hedge funds can perform well even when markets head lower. Market downturns and the subsequent losses suffered by mutual funds have taught institutional investors that hedge funds are quicker to respond and can use changing market conditions to profit more effectively. In fact, hedge funds have even lured many mutual fund managers away, making it a talent-driven industry based on performance. Hedge funds have raised the bar for managers across the financial industry and have actually made the marketplace more efficient and proactive.

Even though the industry has evolved, many small hedge funds like mine will most likely never achieve critical mass. We simply don't have the necessary infrastructure to combat investor skepticism based on the tabloid coverage of a few rotten apples. Nor do we have the capital to stay in business long enough for the tides of public opinion to change and the restrictions to ease up. Those of us with many years of exceptional performance and many wealthy connections might make it, but the average person who dreams of becoming a hedge fund manager has little chance at success. Large funds are able to attract serious capital because money begets money. These funds can afford to build solid teams and infrastructures capable of supporting their ever-increasing capital bases. The small funds get the leftover crumbs—if they're lucky.

While cursing industry regulations under their breath, large funds play along because their size shields them from any harmful effects. Their silence has been bought. Small funds suffer the most from regulations but fear makes them play along, too. They dream of becoming large funds and will not risk making enemies with the mighty SEC so early in their careers. The incredible investment freedom that attracts thousands of people and trillions of dollars to this industry comes at a price: the price of freedom of speech.

For too long, regulations have silenced hedge fund managers like me from detailing our life's work with anyone deemed "financially unworthy." I wish I could've taken out full-page ads about my fund, strategy and performance, which if successful, would've helped me raise large amounts of capital and allowed me to take full advantage of the opportunities placed before me. There's no way to tell whether I would've been successful, but I should've been given the chance. We—the SEC included—need to learn from our failures as much as our successes because the better our understanding of the past, the better prepared we enter the future.

The Numbers

	ANNUAL	RETURNS*	
	S&P 500	PERSONAL ACCOUNT	CILANTRO FUND**
1999	21.04%	910%	
2000	−9.10%	560%	
2001	−11.89%	47%	
2002	−22.10%	98%	
Four-year average	**−5.51%**	**323%**	
2003	28.69%		6.06%***
2004	10.88%		20.37%
2005	4.91%		23.56%
2006			−25.83%
Four-year average	**15.07%**		**6.04%**

*All returns have been fully audited.
**Returns have been adjusted to account for fund fees.
***Fund inception was March 2003.

At press time, Cilantro Fund Partners, LP, owned 1,212,000 restricted shares, Timothy Sykes's family owned 210,000 unrestricted shares, and Timothy personally owned 350,000 restricted shares of Cygnus. Timothy is still stuck leasing his BMW 745Li and his third computer monitor is still broken—there's no downtime in the finance game.

Visit www.timothysykes.com

- To learn about Timothy's instructional trading DVD: **PennyStocking** (BullShip-free, Money-Back Guaranteed)

- To see detailed charts of the trades mentioned (As denoted by the *(t)* icon throughout the book)

- To sign-up to Timothy's Newsletter

- To read Timothy's blog

- To discover Freedom of Finance

- To view Timothy's favorite websites, blogs and books

- To watch exclusive video clips

- To enjoy exclusive offers on future products from BullShip Press

- To read free articles by Timothy and other experts

Printed in the United States
89245LV00007B/173/A